KU-422-637

CONTENTS

	Page
ROME ON FIRE	7
Postscript to Rome on Fire	43
PEACE TALKS IN PALESTINE	45
SHYLOCK'S END	75
Acknowledgments	105

SHYLOCK'S END

AND OTHER PLAYS

BY THE SAME AUTHOR:

Full Length Plays

PETER AND PAUL
THE HOUSE
ISABEL'S ELEVEN
HIPPODROME HILL
BRITANNIA CALLING ⎫ "PLAYS OUT OF TIME"
STEPHEN INTO DICKENS ⎭
THE FIFTH GOSPEL
SHAKESPEARE (*with Clifford Bax*)
EXODUS (*with Halcott Glover*)
CHURCHILL (*with A. J. Talbot*)

One-Act Plays include

WHAT'S WRONG WITH THE DRAMA
    (*Five One-Act Plays*)
OLD BOYHOOD
THE DICKENS OF GRAY'S INN
ISRAEL SET FREE (*Five One-Act Plays*)
JOHNSON WAS NO GENTLEMAN
HATED SERVANTS (*Eight One-Act Plays*)
BERNARD SHAW IN HEAVEN

SIX LONDON PLAYS (*with Vera Arlett*)
UNEARTHLY GENTLEMAN
    A Trilogy of Plays about Shakespeare

SHYLOCK'S END

And Other Plays

by

H. F. RUBINSTEIN

LONDON
VICTOR GOLLANCZ LIMITED
1971

© H. F. Rubinstein 1971

ISBN 0 575 00663 3

Printed in Great Britain by
The Camelot Press Ltd., London and Southampton

ROME ON FIRE

PROLOGUE AND ACT OF A TRAGEDY

To Michael

CHARACTERS

JOSEPHUS ⎫
TACITUS ⎬ *as Chorus*
EUSEBIUS ⎭

ABRAHAM (*Jewish-Christian veteran*)
ESDRAS (*his son*)
SARAH (*wife of Esdras*)
ALEXANDER (*their son*)
ELISSA (*their daughter*)
DRUSILLA (*Roman-Christian, betrothed to Alexander*)
JULIANA (*Jewish-Christian widow*)
DAVID (*her son*)
EUBULUS ⎫
LINUS (*second bishop of Rome*) ⎬ *Non-Jewish friends of Paul*
A NEIGHBOUR (*non-Jewish*) ⎭

PLACE AND TIME

Prologue: *Before the curtain*

Act: *Living room in a Roman apartment house. On a Friday evening in July* A.D. *64*

ROME ON FIRE

Against a dark curtain a long oblong table, set before three empty chairs, faces the audience.

Enter, as Chorus, JOSEPHUS, TACITUS *and* EUSEBIUS, *in that order.* JOSEPHUS, *the youngest in appearance, swarthy, with black hair and beard, well-preserved and dignified, steps briskly to the chair in the centre, courteously signalling his companions to the chairs on either side.* EUSEBIUS, *with snow-white hair and rosy complexion, mild, bespectacled and beaming, seats himself on the far side, while* TACITUS, *wizened, shrewd and gaunt-faced, slips into the nearest chair.* JOSEPHUS, *seeing that they are comfortably settled, rises, and after glancing round the auditorium, bows slightly and opens.*

JOSEPHUS: Spectators, we are three historians of the ancient world, whose names may be known to you. Those who are not interested in the past will not find our conversation interesting. (*He pauses.*) Tacitus, on your left and my right, was born about 55 A.D., in the year of the fourth Roman emperor, Claudius. He died early in the second century, after attaining high honour as a senator, consul and governor of Asia. Eusebius, on my left, historian of the early Christian church, born some 150 years later, in Palestine, became bishop of Caesarea, and an intimate friend of the emperor Constantine the Great, whom he baptized. He died, in his eighties, about 340 A.D. (*A pause.*) I am Flavius Josephus, historian of the Jews, born shortly after the crucifixion of Christ, in the reign of the emperor Caligula. I was one of the leaders in the revolt of my nation against Roman aggression, under the rule of Nero. (*Another pause.*) I am generally regarded as a traitor because, recognizing the hopelessness of further resistance, I defected to the Roman army, then led by Vespasian and his son Titus, both of whom became my friends, and later, in succession, Roman emperors. I always sought to advance the cause of my unfortunate people according to my evaluation of their true interests and destiny. All that is another story. I may not have been a very good man, but it is generally conceded that I was a good historian.

EUSEBIUS: An indispensable historian.

JOSEPHUS (*passing on*): I stand before you, in this company, as the Wandering Jew between Imperial Rome (*bowing to Tacitus*) and the New Order of Christendom (*bowing to Eusebius*). Perhaps I might also profess to stand between the Old and the New Testament.

TACITUS (*testily*): You haven't yet explained what we are all doing here—called from the Shades to make a public show of ourselves!

JOSEPHUS (*patiently*): We have been called as witnesses— expert witnesses, so to speak—in defence of a play claiming to be historical. It purports to make sense of a fragment of history, enacted between the twilight of one world—the world of Tacitus—and the dawn of another, the world of Eusebius. There would seem to be crossroads in history. At one such, we three historians, from our several observation posts, and our different intellectual conditioning, became relatively familiar with aspects of a somewhat chaotic background. Against that background—the background of our play—a group of early Christians, mostly Jews, may be seen (*grimly*) taking what came to them. Only one of the characters—you might call him the hero—

is known to have existed. His name is Linus. Did you ever hear of him, Tacitus?

TACITUS: Linus? Not that I remember.

JOSEPHUS: Nor I—though I could have rubbed shoulders with him, often enough, in the streets of Rome. Eusebius heard of him long after you and I were in our graves.

TACITUS: Who was this fellow Linus, then?

JOSEPHUS: May we have it in your own words, Eusebius? You will find in front of you a recent translation of your *History of the Church.*

EUSEBIUS (*picking up a Penguin*): In a paperback edition!

JOSEPHUS (*complacently*): We are all of us Penguin Classics. (*He exhibits his copy of* The Jewish War.) Yours has an index, by the way.

EUSEBIUS (*who has been vaguely turning the pages*): Oh, thank you. (*He refers to the index.*) "Linus". (*Finding the place.*) Yes, here we are. (*He reads.*) "After the martydom of Paul and Peter, the first man to be appointed Bishop of Rome was Linus."

JOSEPHUS (*to the audience*): Since he places Paul's name before Peter's he probably understood that Paul pre-deceased Peter.

EUSEBIUS (*to himself*): I am, of course, not listening.

JOSEPHUS: As for Linus, we know unequivocally that he was the second man to occupy the chair of Peter. That at least is something.

EUSEBIUS (*racking his memory*): Did I give no further particulars? (*He refers again to the index of his book.*)

JOSEPHUS: Yes, you disclose elsewhere that he remained Bishop of Rome for twelve years. From which we may conclude that he lived to see the triumph of my friends Vespasian and Titus after the capture of Jerusalem and destruction of the Temple: that darkest day in Jewish history.

EUSEBIUS: Did I not also record that Linus was known to the apostle Paul. (*He manages to find the place.*) I did! (*reading*) ". . . mentioned by Paul when writing to Timothy from Rome, in the salutation at the end of the epistle."

JOSEPHUS: Correct. And what does all your information amount to? A blank. Yet this obscure Linus held a key position in the church throughout the most critical and bloodiest ordeal in its whole history. You do not minimize the ordeal, but you leave us to speculate about the kind of man who bore the brunt of it.

EUSEBIUS (*with a sigh*): I cannot deny that. But please bear in mind that it was not till many generations after my demise that a bishop of Rome acquired the status and prestige of the papacy. Not that that excuses me.

JOSEPHUS: We don't even know whether Linus was a Jew or a Graeco-Roman.

EUSEBIUS (*irresistibly*): If only one of his *contemporaries* had left me a clue.

JOSEPHUS: I invited that! And you would certainly not have missed such a clue from Josephus.

EUSEBIUS: Did I ever fail to help myself freely to the fruits of your labours?

JOSEPHUS: Nor ever fail to acknowledge handsomely your indebtedness. I must indeed blame myself—and add to it the reproach of failing to foresee that Christianity would ultimately conquer the Roman Empire.

EUSEBIUS: You are over-modest. You at least had the insight to identify the founder of our religion with the long-awaited Jewish Messiah.

TACITUS (*drily*): Whereas that old fool Tacitus missed the whole point—never took the trouble to look beneath the surface of popular prejudice!

JOSEPHUS: It was none of your business. I would say rather, that the cobbler stuck heroically to his last. Tell me, friend Eusebius, for which of his many virtues do you most venerate our master Tacitus?

EUSEBIUS: I certainly envy most the superb artistry of his writing—a quality in which I was so conspicuously deficient. And you?

JOSEPHUS: His sincerity. (*A pause.*) After that I venerate in him—while slightly resenting—the moral values he upheld, leaving our Judaeo-Christianity little, if anything, to teach him.

TACITUS (*not unaffected by these compliments*): One thing I would gladly have been taught by your co-religionists.

JOSEPHUS: What is that?

TACITUS: To hope. When I remember the supreme confidence with which your people used to walk into the arena—and all that happened after the Great Fire—

JOSEPHUS: Ah, the great fire—now we are coming to it!

EUSEBIUS: That was in A.D. 64, the year Peter was martyred—

JOSEPHUS: And the year Linus was appointed his successor. (*He ruminates.*) The great fire, about which every English schoolboy can tell you one thing: that it inspired the emperor Nero to perform on a musical instrument which was invented some fifteen centuries after his decease. (*The others smile.*) And this brings me to the immediate concern of our conference before the curtain. The historical evidence of what happened during and after the Great Fire is recorded in the pages of those Annals with which the name of Tacitus will ever be associated. (*He fingers his own paperback, then, a little nervously, and with great deference, turns to* TACITUS.) If you please, sir.

TACITUS (*amiably*): My turn—my Penguin, eh? (*He picks up the paperback in front of him.*)

JOSEPHUS (*to the audience*): The curtain will shortly rise to discover the apartment of a family of Jewish Christians in Rome on a Friday evening in July 64. It is the evening of the outbreak. I invite Tacitus to read to us from his immortal description of that fire and the consequences.

TACITUS (*who has been examining the Penguin* Tacitus on Imperial Rome): Someone has been marking this copy. Hm! (*Growling*) So I'm to cut a long story short, is that it? (*More genially*) Well, I will do my best. (*He rises majestically and commences to read. As he warms to his work, we become aware that* TACITUS *was not only a great historian, but also a great orator.*)

"Nero's excesses were overtaken by disaster. Now started the most terrible and destructive fire which Rome had ever experienced. Whether it was accidental or caused by the Emperor's criminal act is uncertain. It began in the Circus where it adjoins the Palatine and Caelian hills. Breaking out in shops selling inflammable goods, and fanned by the wind, the conflagration instantly grew and swept violently over the level spaces. Then it climbed the hills, but returned to ravage the lower ground again. It outstripped every counter-measure. The ancient city's narrow winding streets and irregular blocks encouraged its progress." (*He pauses.*) ". . . . By the sixth day enormous demolitions had confronted the raging flames with bare ground and open sky, and the fire was stamped out. But before panic had subsided or hope revived flames broke out again in the more open regions of the city. This new conflagration caused additional ill-feeling, for people believed that Nero was ambitious to found a new city to be called after himself on the estate where it started. To suppress this rumour, Nero fabricated scapegoats—and punished with every refinement the notoriously depraved Christians (as they were popularly called). Their originator, Christ, had been executed in Tiberius's reign by the governor of Judaea, Pontius Pilatus. But in spite of this temporary set-back, the deadly superstition had broken out afresh, not only in Judaea (where the mischief had started) but even in Rome. All degraded and shameful practices collect and flourish in the capital. First, Nero had self-acknowledged Christians arrested. Then, on their information, large numbers of others were condemned— not so much for incendiarism as for their anti-social tendencies. Their deaths were made farcical. Dressed in wild animals' skins, they were torn to pieces by dogs, or crucified, or made into torches to be ignited after dark to substitute for daylight. Nero provided his gardens for the spectacle. Despite their guilt as Christians, and the ruthless punishment it deserved, the victims were pitied. For it was felt that they were being sacrificed to one man's brutality rather than to the national interest." (*He resumes his seat.*)

JOSEPHUS: End of prologue.

BLACK OUT

ACT

Living room on an upper storey of a Roman apartment house, on a
Friday evening in July A.D. 64.

   Two exits: one, upstage left, leading to the rest of the apart-
ment; the other, down, right, opening from a staircase and
landing. A window in the centre of the back wall commands a
panoramic view over the lower regions of the city and surrounding
hills. Not far from the window, a long table set for an evening
meal with chairs round it. At the right end of the table, a Jewish
menorah *(candelabrum) is noticeable. Beside it a small Roman*
lamp with tinder-box, upon a large tray holding also a decanter of
wine, some bread, a goblet and a dish in readiness for a Sabbath
celebration ritual.

   Assembled family and guests stand about awaiting a summons
to the table from the host, ESDRAS, *and hostess,* SARAH, *who are*
supported by their son, ALEXANDER *and daughter,* ELISSA, *both*
in their twenties, with ALEXANDER's *fiancée,* DRUSILLA, *and a*
red-haired youth, DAVID, *accompanying his mother,* JULIANA,
in near attendance.

SARAH: Should we wait any longer for Linus and Eubulus?
What do you think, Esdras? We are not expecting anyone
else. And they are hardly likely to be coming as late as this.

ESDRAS (*uneasily*): I can't remember their ever keeping us
waiting before.

ELISSA (*pleading*): But they must intend to come, or one of
them would have sent us word! Do let us wait a little
longer, father. They both so love joining in the singing.

SARAH: They would hardly wish us to postpone Kiddush
beyond sunset, Elissa!

DAVID (*betraying impatience*): And the sun must surely be
setting by this time.

SARAH (*turning to the window*): Yes, it is beginning—Oh, look! (*She points.*) That cloud of smoke rising. Over there! It's a fire, I'm afraid.

JULIANA: What, another one. That's the second this week!

SARAH (*watching*): Over by the Circus, as usual. They'll be occurring daily before long.

ELISSA (*hardly listening*): Linus has never been late before.

DAVID (*promptly*): From which it follows, my dear Elissa, that he won't be turning up now.

ELISSA: It doesn't follow—and I'm quite certain they'll both be coming.

DAVID (*primly*): Well, don't let us quarrel about it!

ESDRAS (*shaking his head*): The Sabbath waits for no man, children. (*Deciding.*) Our friends will understand. And they may yet be in time for the singing. Come, Sarah! (*She advances, he hands her the tinder-box, and she kindles the lamp while he murmurs*) "Blessed art thou . . . who has sanctified us by thy commandments and commanded us to kindle the sabbath light." (SARAH *extinguishes the tinder, and goes to her husband who kisses and blesses her. His children are then kissed and blessed in turn.* ESDRAS *continues.*) "And it was evening and it was morning, the sixth day. . . . And on the seventh, God had finished his work and rested. And God blessed the seventh day and hallowed it." (*He pours wine into the goblet, holds it up and pronounces*) "Blessed art thou, O Lord our God, who created the fruit of the vine." (*He sips, then hands the cup to* SARAH *who, after sipping, passes it on to* ALEXANDER *and* ELISSA *who, following the same ritual, pass it on to the other guests, and back to* SARAH *to be replaced on the table. Meanwhile . . .*)

ELISSA: Father.

ESDRAS: Yes, my dear.

ELISSA: Might we not postpone the singing till after supper? (*He looks puzzled.*) To give Linus and Eubulus a chance of joining in.

ESDRAS: If or when they eventually arrive, you mean?

ELISSA: I am sure they will arrive.

ESDRAS: Well, I see no objection. Do you, Sarah?

SARAH: None whatever.

ELISSA (*relieved*): Oh, thank you, father.

ESDRAS (*calling to his son*): Now, Alexander.

ALEXANDER (*coming forward*): "We give thanks unto thee our Father for the holy vine of David, thy servant, which thou hast made known unto us through Jesus thy servant."

THE COMPANY: Amen.

ESDRAS (*taking a portion of bread*): "Blessed art thou, O Lord our God, who bringest forth bread from the earth." (*He breaks the bread into fragments, swallows one, and drops the others into the dish which is then circulated, as, previously, the cup; when all have partaken, the dish is returned to the table. While this is proceeding, the inner door opens and* ABRAHAM, *frail and aged father of* ESDRAS, *emerges, leaning heavily on a stick; makes his way to the table, waving off offers of assistance, while smiling wanly in response to gestures of greeting.*)

SARAH (*to* ESDRAS): Your father's come in.

ESDRAS: Thank God he's well again.

SARAH (*calling*): You told us not to call or expect you, Grandfather, and we took you at your word! (*He nods approval.*) The sleep has restored you? (*He has seated himself*)

*at the table. She brings him the wine and bread, of which he
partakes, mumbling his blessings.*)

ESDRAS: And you have come in time to hear your grand-
daughter recite. (*Calling her.*) Elissa.

ELISSA (*raising her voice*): "We give thanks unto thee, our
father, for the life and knowledge which thou didst make
known to us, though Jesus thy servant. (*Carefully.*) As this
broken bread was scattered upon the tops of the moun-
tains, and, being scattered, became one, so gather thy
church from the ends of the earth unto thy kingdom,
through Jesus Christ."

ALL (*as before*): Amen.

[*General relaxation and exchange of greetings.*

ESDRAS (*above the hubbub*): It has been proposed that we
defer our chanting in the hope that Linus and Eubulus
may yet be joining us. Will that be satisfactory? (*As no one
objects.*) Happy Sabbath!

ALEXANDER (*taking* DRUSILLA *aside*): Drusilla, darling,
father says I may kiss you publicly this evening. (*They
embrace tenderly. It is seen that she is near tears, and onlookers
are affected.*)

DAVID (*cornering* ELISSA): When am I to be allowed such a
privilege, Elissa?

ELISSA: Oh, please not again, David!

DAVID (*desperately*): Can't you be kind to me?

ELISSA: You know I would if I could. (*Escaping.*) I must go
and talk to my grandfather. (*Approaching* ABRAHAM.)
Happy Sabbath, Ancient! (*She kisses him.*) One of your bad
days?

ABRAHAM (*shaking his head*): I have lived too long, child.

ELISSA: The same old nightmares? Is it the brethren in Judea again?

ABRAHAM (*trembling*): I fear for them all the time. I can see no way out.

ELISSA: Then you can do nothing to help. Worrying won't help.

ABRAHAM: We must submit to God's will, yes. But they are our people. My grandfather came from Jerusalem.

ELISSA: Still, worrying won't help.

ABRAHAM: I have lived too long. That is my trouble. (*He pats her head and gradually ceases to tremble.*) And what's your trouble, child?

ELISSA: Mine?

ABRAHAM: What were you so cross about? I was watching you.

ELISSA (*looking away*): Oh, that was nothing.

ABRAHAM: Hm. (*Glancing round.*) Where are Romulus and Remus this evening?

ELISSA: Who? Oh, Linus and Eubulus! (*Mirthlessly*) You funny old man!

ABRAHAM (*as the outer door opens*): And here they come perhaps. (ELISSA *starts up as* EUBULUS *enters: a cultured Roman, in his prime, sensitive, well-balanced, good-humoured, but at present hot and anxious.*)

ESDRAS: Eubulus! (*He hastens forward.*) Welcome indeed! But—without Linus?

EUBULUS (*mopping his brow*): Yes, I must apologize for both of us. I was waiting for Linus at his lodging.

SARAH (*coming forward*): Where is he?

EUBULUS (*uneasily*): Linus has evidently been held up—

ELISSA (*with a gasp*): Held up?

EUBULUS: Or he would have returned to fetch me, as we had arranged.

ELISSA: You mean—you don't *know* where he is?

ESDRAS: Or what can have held him up?

EUBULUS (*with a sigh*): I only wish I could answer your questions.

SARAH: He sent no message?

EUBULUS: None that reached me. It is unlike him, I must admit.

ESDRAS (*quietly*): Somewhat alarming, is it not?

EUBULUS: Disturbing, certainly. But (*with an effort*) I would not say alarming. After all, there could be many different reasons and Linus is well able to take care of himself. (*Bravely.*) As likely as not, he will be arriving here presently, with some perfectly simple explanation and full of contrition—as I am—for disturbing the peace of a Sabbath evening. You did not wait too long for us, I hope?

ESDRAS: We have finished the Kiddush.

EUBULUS: Then let me at least wish everyone present a Happy Sabbath. (*As the others respond,* ELISSA, *struggling with her fears, wanders away, and, catching her grandfather's eye, returns to sit beside him, taking no part in the succeeding conversation.*)
We are a smaller gathering than usual. Are there other absentees?

SARAH (*breaking an embarrassed silence*): My parents will not be coming again.

EUBULUS: What—Rabbi Joshua and his wife? I am sorry to hear that. No illness, I trust—?

ESDRAS (*stiffly*): To our great regret, they have taken exception to the innovations in our liturgy. (*With a sigh.*) We have done what we could to meet their views. We are as concerned as they are to preserve the spirit of all that is beautiful and significant in the traditions. But, after all, as I had to remind them, we are Christians as well as Jews.

EUBULUS: How did they react to that?

ESDRAS: Most unpleasantly.

SARAH: They started abusing Paul—as though his old quarrel with the Eastern synagogues had any bearing on the question.

EUBULUS: You were all in Peter's fold, were you not?

ESDRAS: Long before Paul was more than a name in Rome. Before Paul's advent there was never any serious disharmony. We had our arguments, of course, as every family must, over matters of opinion—even a united Christian family.

DRUSILLA (*dramatically*): Ours was once a united Christian family—before Paul's advent ... (*and she bursts into tears.*)

ALEXANDER (*comforting her*): Dru, darling—you've been so brave about it all!

EUBULUS (*mystified*): Drusilla's family—are they not —as usual—?

SARAH (*with compressed lips*): They also will not be coming again.

DRUSILLA (*between sobs*): They want me to break off our engagement.

EUBULUS (*shocked*): What, with Alex! But for what reason?

ALEXANDER: For the reason to end all reason! Drusilla must not be allowed to marry one of the circumcised!

DRUSILLA (*between sobs*): And they say that anyone who observes a Jewish religious festival—including the Sabbath—must be on the side of Paul's enemies.

SARAH: And they call themselves followers of his— followers of Paul who sat at the feet of Gamaliel!

EUBULUS: I am simply aghast! If Paul were only here to reason with them! (*A silence.*)

JULIANA (*suddenly intervening*): "If!" Yes, if. (*Caustically.*) And if expressions of pious hopes could be expected to bring Paul back to us— (*With determination.*) May I ask Eubulus a simple question?

DAVID (*apprehensive*): Is this a suitable occasion, mother?

JULIANA: Please allow me to exercise my own judgment, David!

EUBULUS (*uncomfortably*): Ask me any question you please, Juliana.

DAVID (*sotto voce*): And now there'll be no stopping her!

JULIANA (*directly*): Who is the present head of our church? That is what I want to know.

EUBULUS (*slowly*): It is unfortunately not possible to answer that question.

JULIANA: Unfortunately, to say the least of it! Esdras regrets that Paul is not here to reason with Drusilla's parents. Where is Paul? Nobody knows. Where is Peter?

Nobody knows that either. How long is it since they were reported missing, one after the other? If we could be offered even a glimmering of hope that either of them would be restored to us! Is nobody else *concerned* about this state of affairs? To be deprived of both the Apostles, while we are still cut off from our brethren in Jerusalem— what is to become of us? We are sheep left without a shepherd! How can a church survive without anyone in authority? We must have a leader!

EUBULUS (*in a low voice*): I agree with those sentiments.

JULIANA: But you don't answer my question!

EUBULUS: For the present, we can only be patient.

JULIANA: I beg to differ. There are alternative courses. You and Linus must have discussed the situation often enough. You are both on the inner council, are you not?

EUBULUS (*patiently*): You might say so.

JULIANA: Then I do say so. And why should not the inner council elect a new chief—a "bishop", or whatever you call it? If there's no other way, you could draw lots for him, as, they say, the first apostles did, when they chose a new man in place of Judas Iscariot.

EUBULUS: Judas was known to have hanged himself.

JULIANA: Ought we not to presume that both Paul and Peter must be dead, after this lapse of time?

EUBULUS: No shred of evidence has come to light— nothing more than rumours.

DRUSILLA: My foolish parents believed the story that Paul had been abducted by Jewish extremists, as the only way to silence him.

JULIANA: Shall I tell you what I think? Someone who shall be nameless was determined to stifle the Christian church and wasn't sure which of our two great leaders was the more important. So he had both of them secretly put out of action. And who knows whether his plan may not have succeeded? Who knows? (*A pause.*)

ESDRAS: Sometimes I ask myself a frightening question, Eubulus. Would it have been better if Paul had never reached Rome?

ALEXANDER: He might have been still living and active. Is that what you mean, father?

DRUSILLA: Could not the same be said about Peter?

JULIANA: May we come back to the point, please? After what we have been hearing, can anyone doubt that the state of our church is desperate, and deteriorating rapidly. (*A pause.*)

ELISSA: Are you asleep, Ancient?

ABRAHAM: No, I am listening.

ELISSA: Are we better off in Rome than your grandfather was in Jerusalem?

ABRAHAM (*reminiscing*): My grandfather was an optimist— and a gambler. He transported the entire family from Jerusalem to Rome when civil wars were raging all over Italy. But Herod the Great was king of Judaea, and my grandfather said, Anything is better than that. (*A pause.*)

SARAH (*calling across the room*): Is your grandfather still comfortable, Elissa?

ABRAHAM: How can I sleep? How can I be comfortable? Leave me to wrestle alone, child.

[*Reluctantly* ELISSA *obeys.* SARAH, *meanwhile, has risen and is moving towards the window.*

SARAH: Oh look! The fires! (*She stares out.*) It's spreading in all directions! (*Raising her voice.*) Come and look everybody!

EUBULUS (*rising*): I heard there was a big fire over by the Circus.

[*The others, with him, gather round the window.*

JULIANA (*awed*): There's never been one as big as this before.

[*All watch for some moments in fascination.*

DAVID (*sliding up to ELISSA, who is staring out*): It's a good way off still. We're well out of it up here!

DRUSILLA (*clinging to ALEXANDER*): Oh Alex, I can't bear to think of all those poor homeless families!

ALEXANDER (*his arm about her*): Come away, darling. (*He leads her back into the room.*)

ELISSA (*dreamily*): "Fire leapt from roof to roof of gods and men."

EUBULUS (*at her side*): Aeneid, Book Four. Poor Dido's funeral pyre.

ELISSA: Vergil has a word for everything.

EUBULUS: You've noticed that too?

ELISSA: The Aeneid is a kind of Bible, isn't it?

DAVID (*rashly*): But Vergil was a pagan writer, remember.

ELISSA (*to EUBULUS*): I think I know Book Four by heart.

EUBULUS: Aeneas and Dido—who could ever forget them?

ELISSA (*as they move away*): All but a perfect story.

EUBULUS: Why "all but"? What's wrong with the story?

ELISSA: Dido. She shouldn't have cursed Aeneas. It was horrible of her.

EUBULUS: Poor Dido, what else could she do?

ELISSA: She could have understood her man—realized that he *had* to leave her. What else could Aeneas do—with a divine mission to fulfil? She was lucky to be loved by such a man for five minutes!

EUBULUS (*rather taken aback*): That's an original notion.

JULIANA (*overhearing*): I'm another Vergil lover. Shall we all sit down again. (*She sits between them.*) My late husband used to say I would have been perfectly happy to be shipwrecked on an uninhabited island if I could have my Vergil with me . . . and of course the Bible.

ALEXANDER (*from a nearby chair*): Who wouldn't choose to live on an uninhabited island—to get away from Rome!

JULIANA: If only it could be Vergil's Rome!

DRUSILLA: Instead of Nero's!

DAVID (*not to be left out of the conversation*): Mind what you're saying! Someone may be listening behind these walls!

EUBULUS (*seriously*): A useful reminder. Informers are known to have been active lately.

DAVID (*glibly*): The favourite dodge, I hear, is for a man to knock at the door, introduce himself as a new tenant, and spin some yarn about his wife running short of milk.

DRUSILLA (*shuddering*): Oh, and I mentioned that man's name! Could I have been heard?

SARAH: Don't worry, Dru! We hear our neighbours' voices only when they are quarreling, and fortunately don't catch the words even then! (*Turning to her husband.*) Esdras, ought we to wait any longer?

ESDRAS: For Linus? I was asking myself the same question. What do others think?

EUBULUS (*no one else volunteering*): Why not put it to the vote?

ELISSA (*definitely*): I intend to wait in any case.

DAVID (*both jealous and hungry*): And if Linus is never seen again?

ELISSA (*recoiling, stricken*): What—what are you saying? (*In distress she wanders back to her grandfather.*) Ancient, I'm in trouble. One of your nightmares.

ABRAHAM (*as best he can*): Sit here, child. (*She obeys.*) We must help one another.

ELISSA: Talk to me about Vergil's Rome, Ancient.

ABRAHAM: The Peace of Augustus? That will not help. That peace was no more than an interlude. The smell of old fears—of war and revolution—was still in the air. And the interlude passed, and the smell has come back. We must live in the Now. And now we must be tough, both you and I, prepare to take what has to come, and, above all, see clearly, without illusions.

ELISSA: That helps. (*She closes her eyes.*) But I cannot see clearly.

ABRAHAM: You must, child. The Peace of Augustus will never return. You must see beyond.

ELISSA (*straining*): Yes. Peace. There is another peace beyond, the peace of Heaven. That is real. I can see clearly.

ABRAHAM: Then you can prophesy.

ELISSA: And now I can see Linus. (*She relaxes.*) Linus is safe. Father, can you hear me? Linus is on his way to us at last.

DAVID (*in mockery*): Perhaps Elissa can tell us what has been keeping him.

ELISSA (*vaguely*): Perhaps I could. (*Haltingly.*) Yes, it was a labour of Hercules.

DAVID (*with an ugly laugh*): First Aeneas—now Hercules! What next?

EUBULUS (*gravely*): It would be in character. I have known Linus since we were boys. He is of truly heroic stature.

ELISSA (*going over to* EUBULUS): Was he unusual as a boy?

[DAVID *pointedly walks away, going over to the window.*

EUBULUS (*quietly effective in the growing restlessness*): His manhood was more interesting. He was always fearless, and the army gave him the discipline he needed. He would have held an important command if he had stayed on. But he had discovered the church. (*A pause.*) He brought me into it. He became a new man, all his energies harnessed like water in a cemented cistern.

ELISSA (*following, rapt*): Not water. It is fire within.

DAVID (*almost hysterically*): Fire within—and (*pointing*) fire without! Fire with a vengeance!

[*The group breaks up, in a return of restlessness.*

SARAH (*going to the window*): You are right. The whole region seems to be enveloped. The wind must be blowing the flames back from the hills.

ELISSA (*calling to her*): We can do nothing about it, mother.

DAVID (*calling back*): Therefore let us eat, drink and be merry!

JULIANA (*sharply*): David! Control yourself!

DAVID (*wildly*): Yes. Then we can go on talking about the great man who we hope will be arriving for supper before the next Sabbath!

[*The outer door is suddenly opened, and* LINUS *appears: a strong man, slightly reeling as if under blows. He closes the door, and stands with his back to it as if uncertain of his bearings.*

EUBULUS (*in extreme relief*): Linus! At last!

LINUS (*unsteadily*): Rather late, am I? They kept me at the baths. (*All stare at him.*)

EUBULUS: The baths?

LINUS: I needed a bath rather badly.

ESDRAS (*advancing*): Are you—quite well?

LINUS: I think so. (*He pulls himself together.*) There's a big fire raging in the lower regions. Does anyone know about it?

SARAH (*coming forward*): We were watching it when you came in.

LINUS (*with a gesture*): Ah, my kind hostess. (*Vaguely.*) May I sit down for a moment? (EUBULUS *leads him to a chair.*) Has everyone been waiting for me? I am so sorry. Yes, I'm quite well.

ESDRAS: The singing was postponed for your benefit by special request.

SARAH: And now shall we all have supper? I am sure Linus must be famished. (*There is a general drift towards the table. Only* LINUS *does not stir.*) Will you not come to our table?

LINUS: What? (*He half rises.*) Not to eat, please. I couldn't touch any food yet.

SARAH (*stupidly*): You have had your supper already? (*He shakes his head.*)

ELISSA (*gently*): Mother, dear, I think a cup of wine might revive him. Wait! (*She goes swiftly to the table, fills a cup from a decanter of wine and, returning, hands it to* LINUS, *who drains it in one gulp.*) Shall I fill it again? (*Mutely he returns the cup to her.*) Mother, dear, Linus would like to be left in peace, I think. Could we start supper? (*She hurries away with the cup.*)

SARAH (*taking the point*): Will everyone please come to the table? (*No further persuasion is needed.*)

EUBULUS (*to* SARAH): May Linus and I join you later?

[*As* SARAH *bustles away to preside at the table,* ELISSA *comes back with two filled cups which she hands to* LINUS *and* EUBULUS *in turn.*

ELISSA (*withdrawing quickly*): I'll bring something to eat presently. (*Back at the table she assists her mother in circulating plates etc.*)

ESDRAS (*seeing everyone seated*): Shall we be silent for a moment?

[*All at the table rise and murmur a short grace with him.* LINUS *and* EUBULUS *remain silent until the company have resumed their seats, and the meal has begun.*

EUBULUS (*quietly*): You won't want to talk yet, and I have guessed the worst from your eyes. At least there is certainty now.

LINUS (*half-choking*): I have seen both graves. (*He lowers his head, and for some moments shakes convulsively, then quickly recovers.*)

EUBULUS: Only the future matters.

C

LINUS: No. Only the present. The future will depend on it. (*A pause.*) No, don't say anything. (*With a change of tone.*) That message was no hoax, by the way. The woman was waiting for me, and I followed her for miles. Then I followed the man who relieved her—until he was relieved by another. I thought there would be no end of them. But the end came. At the deathbed of an old legionary who'd served under me, and was able to spit out his message, and hand me this. (*He produces a tattered paper.*) Read it.

EUBULUS (*recoiling*): *His* handwriting! Li!

LINUS: Yes. Legible—and short. Read it. (EUBULUS *obeys, and hands it back to him, unable to speak.*) Yes, Bul, you are sitting beside the successor of Blessed Peter. (*He closes his eyes.*)

EUBULUS: One prayer is answered, then. Our most immediate need has been met. In the only possible choice. A guided choice. It must be announced. (*He half-rises.*)

LINUS: Not just yet, Bul. (*A longish silence, both praying.*) Ah! (*He sees* ELISSA *approaching with a tray.*)

EUBULUS: Providence prevents!

ELISSA (*placing her tray on a chair*): May I fill the cups? (*She proceeds to do so.*)

EUBULUS (*eyeing the tray*): You would tempt us to break our fasts?

ELISSA: Please. (*He helps himself from her selection of eatables.*)

EUBULUS (*after tasting*): Strongly recommended, Linus!

ELISSA (*before* LINUS, *shyly*): Will you not try?

LINUS (*abruptly*): Of course I will! (*He falls to it without more ado.*)

ELISSA (*hovering*): Another one! (*He obliges her. Satisfied, she shoulders her tray, and returns to the table.*)

LINUS (*watching her*): There goes a true daughter of Israel.

EUBULUS: Elissa! She's very much in love with you. Did you know that?

LINUS: I thought she was betrothed to that red-haired youth.

EUBULUS (*drily*): Nothing could be more remote from the case.

LINUS: Oh. (*Looking at the assembled guests.*) We are a smaller company than usual.

EUBULUS: Alas! (*He sighs.*) Yes. Defectors of both brands: sticklers for orthodoxy at one end, anti-Judaizers at the other. A menacing problem in miniature.

LINUS: Confound all extremists! We shall have to steer a consistent middle course, at all costs.

EUBULUS: It won't be easy, the way things are going. Has it occurred to you, Li, that even these innocent Friday night family parties could become a stumbling-block, under irresistible pressure?

LINUS: There are no certainties in life, Bul, but I don't think either you or I could ever be persuaded to break faith with Jerusalem.

EUBULUS: You and I will not live for ever, Linus.

LINUS: And that's true too. (*He rises abruptly.*) Come, you must be almost as hungry as I am. (*He marches to the table, with* EUBULUS *following, and finds a seat next to* ELISSA *which he occupies.*) Elissa! (*She looks up, startled.*) You met Elijah in the wilderness. (*She is speechless.*) "An angel touched him and said 'arise and eat'."

ELISSA (*confused*): Let me serve you, please. (*She proceeds to do so.* EUBULUS *has seated himself next to* SARAH *who is looking after him. Eating and drinking goes on quietly.*)

ABRAHAM (*breaking the silence*): "Yea, though I walk through the valley of the shadow of death, I will fear no evil."

SARAH (*happening to glance out of the window*): Merciful God, what a conflagration!

LINUS (*thinking aloud*): And that is the evil I will not fear. Fire out of control. "For thou art with me." (*Raising his voice.*) We keep to the middle of the road, Eubulus! "With thy rod and thy staff to comfort me"—in this city of doom!

ESDRAS: In the midst of such highly inflammable material as a Roman mob.

ALEXANDER: With a mad Caesar to inflame it!

JULIANA (*with a slight giggle*): A Caesar whose glamorous wife, for all her Jewish leanings, is not above suspicion!

EUBULUS: Let us stick to the text. "Thou preparest a table before me in the midst of mine enemies—"

[*There is a sudden knock at the outer door. All freeze, and anxious glances are exchanged.* ESDRAS *rises.*

ESDRAS (*going to the door*): Who is there? What do you want? (*A muffled reply is just audible. Opening the door.*) I can't hear you.

[*A respectable-looking citizen enters. Mutual inspection.*

CITIZEN: We've met on the stairs, I think. I live next door.

ESDRAS: What can I do for you?

NEIGHBOUR: A neighbourly service, if you will. My wife thought you might be so kind. We're in a difficulty. Some old friends called unexpectedly, and the fact is we are a bit short of bread. We thought you might have a loaf or two to spare.

ESDRAS (*turning to his wife*): Sarah?

SARAH (*rising to the occasion*): I could let you have a few rolls, if that would do.

NEIGHBOUR: Most kind of you.

SARAH: I'll fetch them from the larder. (*She goes out at once. A pause.*)

NEIGHBOUR: Shocking fire out there. (*He advances a step.*) Lucky we're living well out of the way. (*He moves further forward.*) And a good view of everything into the bargain! (*He turns from the window to glance at the table.*) Looks as if I've been intruding on some kind of a feast. (*A slight pause.*) A religious ceremony, perhaps?

ESDRAS (*evenly*): It is the evening of a Jewish Sabbath.

NEIGHBOUR: I've heard of all that. It's a Christian ceremony, I know.

ESDRAS: A Jewish ceremony, sir.

NEIGHBOUR: Isn't that the same thing?

[SARAH *reappears at that moment.*

ESDRAS: Here is your bread, sir.

NEIGHBOUR (*inspecting objects on the table*): And there's bread. Bread and wine, I see. For sacramental purposes, perhaps.

ESDRAS: Yes, for the celebration of our Sabbath. That *Menorah*, as we call it, is a small replica of the great golden candelabrum in the temple of Jerusalem, where our family come from. We light the candles for our Chanucah Festival.

NEIGHBOUR: Your family? (*He examines their faces.*)

ESDRAS: We have belonged to the Jewish Community of Rome for three generations. This is my father, my wife, my son, my daughter—(*indicating each in turn*).

NEIGHBOUR: And this gentleman? (*He fixes* LINUS.) Is he a member of the Jewish community?

ELISSA (*plunging in*): Of course. He is one of the family— (*in a tense silence*) just as you might say (*with a smile*) that our emperor Nero is a member of the family of *his* Jewish wife. Cornelius (*taking* LINUS'*s arm*) happens to be my husband.

NEIGHBOUR: I see. (*Appreciatively.*) That's good! (*With a wink.*) Well, we know all about Lady Poppaea!

ELISSA (*deadpan*): Who I believe is a very beautiful woman.

NEIGHBOUR (*grinning back*): That's a matter of taste, as you might say. (*He prepares to leave.*) But I mustn't keep you all from your supper.

ESDRAS: You are forgetting the bread, sir.

NEIGHBOUR: So I was! (*Taking it from* SARAH.) And thank you for helping us out with it. (*He clears his throat.*) We all know there are good Jews as well as bad Jews. If his religion's respectable I wouldn't hold it against any man. Only you hear some funny things nowadays.

ELISSA: And you can't believe everything you hear, either.

NEIGHBOUR: Just what I say! Well, good health to all! (*And he retires sheepishly, releasing the tension. But before anyone can speak,* ESDRAS, *holding up a hand, goes to the door, opens it gently, peers out, and, closing it again, utters a fervent* "Thank God", *amid sighs of relief. Only* ELISSA *stands aloof, shamefaced.*)

EUBULUS: We have had fair warning. We are sheep among wolves, and must be cunning as serpents. (*Observing* ELISSA's *plight.*) But Elissa, you were marvellous—such presence of mind! And what an actress! (*But* ELISSA *has fled from the room.*) Will somebody bring Elissa back, please. I have an important announcement to make—if Linus permits. (*Turning to him.* LINUS *nods briefly.*)

SARAH: Leave Elissa to me. (*She goes resolutely after her.*)

EUBULUS (*as all wait in expectation*): Dear Elissa!

LINUS: But for her improvisation, I might have betrayed all of us. I was off my guard.

[SARAH *returns with* ELISSA, *who is now composed and smiling.*

ELISSA: I apologize for my idiotic behaviour, but no more compliments, please! The incident may be regarded as closed, I hope.

EUBULUS: Subject to one—and only one—comment, which arises out of the incident. (*Impressively.*) Among this little group of Christians who, thanks to a young woman's wit, have been preserved from the snare of the fowler, there happens to be included (*he waves to* LINUS) the new bishop of the church of Rome. (*A gasp of astonishment goes up.*) Do not ask me tonight to give you more than bare facts. (*Slowly.*) It is now known for certain that the blessed Apostles Peter and Paul—both of them—suffered martyrdom, and are no longer alive on earth. It is also known for certain that blessed Peter, before he passed on, appointed our brother

Linus to succeed him. There is nothing more I can put into words. (*He falls on his knees. Others follow his example in the ensuing silence.*)

ABRAHAM (*breaking the silence*): "Blessed be the Lord God of Israel for he hath visited and redeemed his people." (*A chorus of Amens.*)

EUBULUS (*rising*): Linus—if you feel like it.

[*The others have risen.*

LINUS (*after a moment*): I am not a man of words. If I have any gifts that qualify me for the office of your bishop, they are the gifts of a well-trained soldier. I think they will be needed. I have had my orders, and I shall obey them— and I ask for your prayers and your trust on those terms. (*A pause.*) Anything else? Yes, one thing, which you may tell me is out of place. On this strange occasion, I am conscious of extreme loneliness. And I remember that God has said, "It is not good that the man should be alone. I will make him an help meet for him." (*He pauses.*) I have much to learn about the duties of a bishop, but I am aware of no law which obliges me to remain celibate. I need a partner, and for a special task I have set myself, I need a partner of a special quality. My predecessor was a Jew and my task will be to maintain the unity between Jew and Gentile in a church founded by Jews to bring the rest of the world to their God. There is a danger that our church may forget the cause of its origin. I hope to avert that danger. (*Another pause, and he turns solemnly to* ESDRAS.) It is your custom to welcome the Sabbath as a bridegroom greets his bride. If your daughter, whom I love, will take the risk, I ask for her hand in marriage.

[*A stunned silence, during which* DAVID, *in dejection, after a hurried exchange of whispers with his mother, detaches himself and slinks noiselessly out of the apartment.*

ESDRAS (*at length*): What have you to say to this, Elissa?

ELISSA (*taut*): I have to impose a condition. Yes, I will declare it publicly. (*She pauses.*) The risk is greater for Linus. I would run any risk for his sake, and I love him whatever happens. But, whatever happens, the church comes first. Those are the orders which he must obey. I could not marry Linus without the assurance that whenever our marriage becomes a hindrance to the church, he will consent to my releasing him.

LINUS: How could it ever—? (*He checks himself, aghast at the thought.*)

ELISSA: (*turning to* ABRAHAM): Ancient, can you see into the future for us? (*His body is convulsed.*) Yes, strain that inner eyesight! What can you see?

ABRAHAM: The burning fiery furnace.

ELISSA: There have been burning fiery furnaces before, and men cast into the midst of them have emerged unscathed.

LINUS: Those men were tested, and the fires burnt themselves out.

ELISSA: And the men have survived, as Linus will survive.

LINUS: The church will survive. I'll answer for that.

ABRAHAM: There is God's Word for it.

ELISSA (*with a cry*): But what sort of church will it be, when the fires of Rome have burnt themselves out and the smouldering Judaean fires have died down—as die down they will in due season? Will this Christian church ever be the same again?

ABRAHAM: All things in life must change.

ELISSA: Even old loyalties, torn asunder—(*she covers her face*).

LINUS: Love and the Will of God will not change.

ELISSA: But man forgets! Did Aeneas forget Dido? It may be. But this I know, and swear, Linus. I shall not complain, when you dismiss me. We may be reunited in the end. (*She is weeping a little, and he cannot reach her. At last she raises her head.*) Yes, I will marry you, Linus—if the offer still holds. Glory be to God—come what may!

[*They embrace tenderly. Salutations and demonstrations of affection from outsiders become unavoidable.*

LINUS (*releasing* ELISSA): May we now have our songs of praise?

ESDRAS: Let us first close the shutters.

SARAH (*at the window*): It is like daylight still. Will they ever have that fire under control? (*She closes the shutters, and the room is almost in darkness.*)

ESDRAS: At last the Sabbath peace. Let us stand back in ourselves, empty out all ugly memories of the past, and imaginings of the future. In patience possess your souls . . .

ABRAHAM (*in a quavering voice*): Let us now give thanks, as Jesus the Messiah in his home in Nazareth gave thanks for the Sabbath.

[ESDRAS *leads the chanting of Psalm 95—"O come, let us sing unto the Lord"—in which all take part.*

CURTAIN

Postscript to

ROME ON FIRE

THIS PLAY—seemingly part of an unfinished tragedy—may appear, paradoxically, to have a happy ending, in the romantic sense. For this reason, I would underline what I mean by describing it as "Prologue and Act of a Tragedy".

The play was conceived, originally, as a tragedy in three acts, all to take place in the same room, with the following time-sequence:

Act One ("Rome on Fire") July 64 A.D.
Act Two ("Jerusalem Falls") Autumn 70 A.D.
Act Three ("Roman Triumph of Vespasian and Titus")
    Autumn 71 A.D.

The story, as it unfolded, was to have shown the gradual breakdown—under pressure of events, and war-fever, resulting from the Jewish revolt in Palestine—of the marriage between Linus and Elissa, "arranged" in Act One. The personal tragedy would reflect, symbolically, the breach between Judaism and Christianity, which some have seen as one of the forgotten tragedies of world history.

After drafting Act One, I decided—hopefully—that the argument of the play, on both levels, could be adequately conveyed, by implication, in a single act, preceded by a Shavian prologue designed to focus the historical background to the perspective of a modern audience.

One theme of the play was suggested by a performance of *The Trojans* at Covent Garden. It occurred to me that the myth of Aeneas and Dido (tragical because Aeneas, to fulfil his destiny as founder of Rome, had to desert Dido) might be relevant to the case of a Linus and Elissa—star-crossed lovers, with a difference—married over-hastily, perhaps.

H. F. R.

PEACE TALKS IN PALESTINE

A HISTORIE IN ONE ACT

*To John,
and his mother,
remembered*

CHARACTERS

KING RICHARD THE FIRST OF ENGLAND (*aged 35*)

BERENGARIA OF NAVARRA, *his wife*

JOANNA, DOWAGER QUEEN OF SICILY, *his elder sister*

HUBERT WALTER, *Bishop of Salisbury*

RAMBAM (or Moses ben Maimon), *a doctor* (*aged 57*)

BLONDEL, *King Richard's minstrel, a troubadour*

ABDAL, *a dervish*

PLACE: *King Richard's tent by Jaffa, Palestine*

TIME: *Late summer,* A.D. *1192*

"*It was in Cairo that Moses ben Maimon settled as physician to Saladin himself. On one occasion, during the course of the Third Crusade, he was invited by Richard Cœur-de-Lion to return to England in his service. But Cairo held the greater attraction for him.*"

CECIL ROTH
A Short History of the English People

PEACE TALKS IN PALESTINE

The spacious tent of KING RICHARD THE FIRST OF ENGLAND, *on a hot summer morning. The* KING, *stricken with fever, lies naked beneath a sheet on a bed of modest dimensions at the rear of the tent. Near the foot of the bed, his young Spanish wife,* BERENGARIA, *and his sister,* JOANNA, *widowed Queen of Sicily, are seated, watching him tensely. In the foreground near the entrance to the tent* (down left) RICHARD'*s minstrel,* BLONDEL DE NESLE, *plays softly on his harp. Beside him sits an inconspicuous attendant wearing the patched robe of a dervish. Trestle tables are within the* KING'*s reach on either side; and nearby a wash-hand stand with basin and ewer. Chests of various sizes are scattered about the tent, some serving as chairs.* BLONDEL *strikes three chords on his harp and ceases. A breathless silence.*

BLONDEL (*lowering his harp*): The King sleeps.

BERENGARIA (*in a whisper*): Is it possible? So quickly. (*She rises and bends over the bed.*) Oh, what a relief! This Blondel is a magician, Joanna.

JOANNA: And Richard depends on his music at all times. (*Turning to Blondel.*) You have been up with my brother all night, Blondel. Will you not go and rest now.

[BLONDEL *rises unsteadily.*

BERENGARIA: But if Richard should wake, and the fever return. . . .?

JOANNA: Blondel will be within call, I assure you.

BLONDEL (*indicating the dervish*): Abdal will know where to find me, Madam.

JOANNA: As promptly as he found the Queen and me before dawn! But let us hope, for everybody's sake, that Richard will now have a good long sleep. And you too, Blondel.

[BLONDEL *bows low and withdraws from the tent.*

BERENGARIA: Oh Joanna, I have been in such terror!

JOANNA: Richard can be very violent—in delirium especially.

BERENGARIA (*with a shudder*): I must try and forget—at least, it is all over now.

JOANNA: I doubt it. The fever will last a day or two longer yet, I fear.

BERENGARIA: But the crisis is past.

JOANNA: Don't be too sure.

BERENGARIA: He should have allowed me to call a doctor.

JOANNA: Richard will never allow that. He'd rather die. And don't you imagine that Richard, ill or well, is ever going to be cured of a violent nature. But Blondel is better for him than all the doctors. He understands Richard's moods, which is more than I ever did or shall.

BERENGARIA (*wistfully*): I shall never be able to endure violence.

JOANNA: Oh, you'll get used to it, I expect. What is so damnable is that Richard should have fallen sick just at this time—when peace was almost in sight. Richard must reach England before the winter.

BERENGARIA: So everyone keeps saying.

JOANNA: And don't you understand? Do you not know what is happening in your husband's kingdom?

BERENGARIA: Only that Count John is making mischief, as usual. After all that Richard has done for him! I think your brother John must be the most ungrateful wretch in all the world!

JOANNA: And is that all you know about Richard's troubles?

BERENGARIA: Richard never tells me anything.

JOANNA (*unkindly*): And does that surprise you?

BERENGARIA: What do you mean? Is it my fault?

JOANNA: Do you encourage Richard to confide in you? You are so easily shocked, my dear!

BERENGARIA (*stiffly*): You are referring again, perhaps, to the scandal about that Faulconbridge—the man Richard knighted at Acre?

JOANNA: Richard confessed to you frankly that he had fathered the man's son . . .

BERENGARIA (*pouting*): Confessed? He boasted of it—and even described the lady's body in detail.

JOANNA: Expecting you to be amused.

BERENGARIA: Adultery does not amuse me, unfortunately. It simply nauseates me!

JOANNA: It is certainly unfortunate—for both of you. (*After a pause, more kindly.*) Did you imagine it would be an easy task to make yourself a suitable wife for the greatest king and bravest soldier in Christendom?

BERENGARIA (*miserably*): Nobody prepared me for it. (*She begins to weep.*) And I thought Richard loved me. I have much to learn, it seems.

JOANNA (*bluntly*): You have. And not much time to learn it in. It might be more sensible to prepare yourself for widowhood.

BERENGARIA: That is a cruel thing to say! I know you despise me—both you and Richard—and I know I am not worthy of him. Yet I do love him—truly—with all his faults.

JOANNA (*sincerely*): How could any woman not love him?

BERENGARIA: And, after all (*her trump card*) Richard did break off his engagement to the French King's sister on my account.

JOANNA (*brutally*): Who told you that? Our mother Elinor, I suppose.

BERENGARIA: Is it not true?

JOANNA: So you never heard the sad story behind that broken engagement? You did not know that the bride-to-be had born a bastard child to our father?

BERENGARIA (*horrified*): Your father? Richard's father? King Henry?

JOANNA: All England knew she was my father's mistress. And Philip of France knew it too—or he might not have taken the jilting of his sister so complacently.

[BERENGARIA *is speechless.*

Yes, you have married into a most unholy family, my poor lamb. But you seem to be completely ignorant of life in this wicked world of ours. Have you received no education outside the children's nursery?

BERENGARIA (*with dignity*): Only the education of a Christian princess. Is that so unfitting for the wife of a Crusader?

[*She breaks off at a sound from the bed behind her.* RICHARD *has stirred slightly in his sleep. Both women look round apprehensively and wait.*

He is still sleeping.

JOANNA (*as a Crusader in full battle-dress enters the tent*): And here is Hubert Walter.

HUBERT (*in his fifties, grave and care-worn*): Save both your ladyships. (*Regarding the sleeping figure.*) All's quiet, then, for the moment.

BERENGARIA: You haven't come to disturb Richard?

HUBERT: That would be folly indeed, madam. Let the King sleep on. The man outside can wait.

JOANNA (*sharply*): What man? Who is it, Hubert?

HUBERT: From the enemy.

JOANNA: From Saladin? (*He nods.*) Were you expecting him?

HUBERT (*shaking his head*): Saladin has been expecting an envoy from us! The King should have replied to his last message three days ago. It might have clinched the argument. (*Pacing restlessly.*) We held all the counters. And now . . .! This setback could hardly have occurred more inopportunely.

JOANNA: I was saying the same thing to the Queen, was I not?

HUBERT (*still pacing*): If we miss the tide again . . .! (*He halts, clenches his teeth.*) The war must be stopped.

JOANNA: Yes. (*With a half-laugh.*) That's what we were all saying last October after the victory at Acre. And we could have had peace then, if my brother hadn't made impossible demands.

HUBERT (*discreetly*): He had set his heart on recovering Jerusalem.

JOANNA: And what use would it have been to us? Were the Crusaders from other lands likely to remain behind merely to preserve our gains? Saladin would have walked in again, as soon as our backs were turned!

HUBERT: There were other difficulties. But the opportunity should not have been allowed to slip.

RICHARD: (*drowsily, opening his eyes*): It was all my sister's fault.

JOANNA (*taken aback*): Richard! (*Flaring up.*) How dare you say that!

BERENGARIA (*excitedly*): Are you awake, my precious? (*She hastens to him.*) Let me make you comfortable. (*She rearranges the pillows, and helps to raise his head.*) How are you feeling, Richard?

RICHARD: Thirsty. (*She pours from a jug, and hands him the cup, from which he drinks.*) Filth! (*He replaces the cup on the side table.*) It was my sister, I say, who wrecked the peace negotiations after Acre.

JOANNA: What a monstrous lie!

RICHARD (*his voice strengthening*): The difficulties Hubert spoke of could have been smoothed out in my peace plan, which she murdered. Saladin's brother, the best loved man in Palestine, would have received the whole of the disputed territories as a dowry on his marriage with the Queen of Sicily, my sister. He and Joanna were to have lived in Jerusalem, guaranteeing freedom of access to all Holy places, for Christians and Moslems alike. It was a master plan which would have made everybody happy.

JOANNA (*fuming*): A Christian Queen was to be happy as the wife of an Infidel! Unheard of!

RICHARD: And none the worse for that! Safardim might even have become a Christian if you'd spoken kindly to him—instead of flying off the handle!

JOANNA: Neither Saladin nor his brother took your mad proposal seriously, as it happened.

HUBERT (*his nerves on edge*): Is this a time for recriminations? By your leave, Madam— May I be heard, Your Majesty?

RICHARD: Yes, Hubert. Partly because I am too weak to argue with my sister—but principally because you are the man on whom I depend to bring me back to England, to settle with brother John.

HUBERT (*grimly*): If we have not left it all too late.

RICHARD: What does that mean? Is there more news from England?

HUBERT: Yes, Sir. Bad news. I hesitate to impart it.

RICHARD (*coldly*): I command you to impart it. And the worse the news—let me assure you—the better for my health.

HUBERT: All, Sir, is summed up by William Bishop of Ely, your Chief Justiciar, who writes that unless you come home at once—*at once*, he stresses—your brother will have usurped not only your authority, but your kingdom.

RICHARD (*pulling himself together*): We will now settle with Saladin. I have studied his last note. He shall have my counter proposals before nightfall.

HUBERT (*in dismay*): Counter proposals, Sir?

RICHARD: Of course. Saladin sued for peace. I offered him terms, which he rejected, proposing other terms in substitution.

HUBERT (*protesting*): With respect, he did not reject your terms, Sir—merely made certain reservations.

RICHARD (*darkening*): One being that I should cede him Ascalon, which I will not do.

HUBERT: Sir, unless he holds Ascalon, Jerusalem is cut off from Egypt.

RICHARD (*raising his voice*): He shall not have Ascalon.

HUBERT: Is that your last word, Sir?

RICHARD: Send for my secretary.

HUBERT: Sir, I must now report— (*he hesitates*) that Saladin's envoy is outside this tent, waiting to see you.

RICHARD (*roaring*): *What?* Why was I not told of his arrival?

HUBERT: Because you were asleep.

RICHARD (*more calmly*): Waiting outside? (*He chuckles.*) So Saladin is impatient! How long has he been waiting? But no matter—let him wait! No one will have told him of my sickness, I trust.

HUBERT: You may be sure of that, Sir. We have taken every precaution, naturally.

RICHARD: So Saladin thinks he can force my hand! Fortunately we know that his need for peace is no less pressing than ours. Who is this envoy?

HUBERT: No one known to me. Not a fighting man, by his look. I could get nothing out of him.

RICHARD: Well, we shall see. (*He considers a moment.*) I am now awake. We'll have him in. Yes, Hubert, now, at once.

[HUBERT *salutes and withdraws.*

BERENGARIA (*timidly*): Richard, my love—you are not fit enough—

RICHARD (*hardly listening*): Am I not?

BERENGARIA: You said you were too weak to argue with Joanna.

RICHARD: That was long ago. (*With a laugh.*) And there's medicine on the way! Mark my words. . . .

[*The tent flap opens, and* HUBERT *reappears, conducting* MOSES BEN MAIMON, *known in his lifetime as* RAMBAM, *and, later, as* MAIMONIDES. *A man in his fifties, turbanned and bearded, with a quietly commanding personality. He carries a large basket.*

HUBERT (*presenting him to the King*): The name is Rambam, Your Majesty. (*He stands aside, impressively.*)

RICHARD (*courteously*): You come from Sultan Saladin—our friend the enemy.

RAMBAM (*bowing*): Who sends his compliments to Your Majesty.

RICHARD: You left him in good health, I hope.

RAMBAM: In better health than you, Sir, I fear.

RICHARD (*evenly*): Oh? Let me at once set your fears at rest. Though you find me idling in bed—after sleeping off the aftermath of my late victory—you may report to your master that I am in excellent condition for resuming hostilities. A recent project for returning to my kingdom has, for good reasons, been set aside. I now propose to spend the winter in Palestine, and pursue my campaign for the recapture of Jerusalem next spring. In short, Sir, unless I am mistaken, you have come to me on a fruitless errand.

RAMBAN (*quietly*): You are mistaken, Sir.

RICHARD (*taken aback*): How so?

RAMBAM: I have neither commission nor authority to discuss peace terms with you.

[*A stunned silence.* HUBERT *is visibly shaken.*

RICHARD: What, then, is your mission?

RAMBAM (*simply*): I am Saladin's doctor. He heard you were unwell.

[RICHARD *emits a short laugh, as* HUBERT, *with a muttered exclamation, stalks angrily away, to retire, presently, into a corner of the tent.* RAMBAM *remains imperturbable.*

RICHARD (*touched in spite of himself*): Your master is the pattern of chivalry. But I do not like doctors. (*He eyes the basket with distaste.*) And you have brought your instruments with you, I see.

RAMBAM (*unruffled*): In this basket? (*He smiles.*) No, Sir. This is a present from my master—a token of his sincere regard for you. (*He advances with it.*) May I place it at your side? (*He deposits the basket on the vacant side-table.*) And open it for you? (*He does so.*) You will see that I have not come on a fruitless errand.

[*The basket is now wide open.*

RICHARD (*licking his lips*): Fruit! (*He peers into the basket.*) Irresistible!

BERENGARIA (*warningly*): Richard! Do not touch any of it! (*As he stretches out a hand, she springs up to prevent him, but he forestalls her.*) Put down that pear at once! (*She tries to snatch it from him.*)

RICHARD (*pushing her aside as he bites into it*): Delicious! (*To RAMBAM.*) Forgive my beautiful Berengaria for suspecting your master of wanting to poison me. We have only been married a few months, and she knows no better. (*Munching the pear.*) The other lady, by the way, is my sister, Dowager Queen of Sicily, the most eligible heiress of the Western world, as I keep reminding everybody.

JOANNA (*rising in wrath*): My brother, as you see, Sir, is still light-headed from his fever. He has been very seriously ill, and if you can help to restore him to health and sanity, we shall all be greatly obliged to you. (*She sweeps out of the tent without more ado.*)

RICHARD (*to* BERENGARIA): Are you not going to follow her?

BERENGARIA: Do you want me to? (RICHARD *shrugs.*) Your mother, I have heard, would not leave your bedside night or day, when you were sick.

RICHARD: My wife is not my mother.

BERENGARIA (*with dignity*): It is my privilege to remain.

RICHARD: These womenfolk have been pestering me to see a doctor in order that I may be bled and purged like other decent Christians. Do you practise these abominations?

RAMBAM: No, Sir—except in cases of emergency.

RICHARD: Do you torment your patients with strong drugs?

RAMBAM: Never, Sir. They do more harm than good.

RICHARD (*less unfriendly*): And what, according to your notions, does good?

RAMBAM: Whatever satisfies the needs of the constitution.

RICHARD: How do you discover those needs?

RAMBAM: By methodical observation and reason.

RICHARD (*after a pause*): How do you assess my constitution?

RAMBAM (*blandly*): All the world knows that you have the heart of a lion.

RICHARD: And how do you treat a lion who has been laid low by this accursed fever? (*He peers into the basket, and carefully selects a peach.*)

RAMBAM (*as he bites it*): You have answered your own question, Sir. Taste is the best physician.

RICHARD: What else do you recommend?

RAMBAM: Cleanliness, fresh air, good company.

RICHARD (*impressed*): You can certainly give points to the medical fraternity of my country.

RAMBAM: Arab-trained doctors are the best in the world, I think.

RICHARD: And I like a man who takes a proper pride in his own nation's achievements.

RAMBAM (*promptly*): I am not an Arab, Sir.

RICHARD: You surprise me. What are you, then?

RAMBAM: A Jew. My right name is Moses ben Maimon.

RICHARD: I would never have guessed it. (*Returning to the basket.*) Another of those pears, I think. (*As he chews it.*)

Some of my best friends in England have been of your persuasion.

RAMBAM: You surprise me in turn, Sir. In all the countries I have so far lived in, my people's best friends have been Moslems.

RICHARD (*continuing to munch*): You have lived in many countries, then?

RAMBAM (*shortly*): Many, Sir.

[*A pregnant silence.*

BERENGARIA (*brightly*): I remember meeting once, in my father's court, a Jewish merchant who was reputed to be quite rich. (*She dries up.*)

RAMBAM: Your Majesty was a Spanish princess, I believe.

BERENGARIA: Yes, Sir. From Navarra.

RAMBAM: I also come from Spain. I was born in Cordoba.

RICHARD: And received your medical training there?

RAMBAM: No, Sir. I was only a boy when we were obliged to leave Cordoba.

HUBERT (*who, tired of sulking, has strolled over from his corner*): That would have been when the Almohads captured the town?

RAMBAM: Yes, Sir. We were given she choice between conversion to Islam and expulsion. My father chose exile for all the family.

RICHARD (*cheerfully*): So that was the beginning of your travels?

[*He continues, in the speeches that follow, to pick out and consume one piece of fruit after another.*

HUBERT (*complacently*): You Jews are well-seasoned travellers.

RAMBAM: Well, we are kept on the move, in the Diaspora.

RICHARD (*his mouth full*): What's a Diaspora? Never heard of it. Do you know the word, Hubert?

HUBERT: It is of Greek derivation, by the sound of it.

RAMBAM (*quietly*): It means the dispersion of the Jews outside the Holy Land.

BERENGARIA (*innocently*): Oh, do you also call it a Holy Land? (*Looking round.*) Have I said something stupid?

HUBERT (*sententiously*): The Jews, Madam, are children of Abraham in the flesh, as we of Abraham in the spirit.

RICHARD: I like the sound of that. (*He helps himself to another peach.*)

BERENGARIA: Of course. I remember now.

RAMBAM: So you see, we are all related, Madam. We have even the same Father in Heaven.

BERENGARIA: Yes. How interesting. Could we not offer the doctor a drink, Richard?

RICHARD: If we had anything worth offering! Lukewarm wine or tepid juice of oranges: which would you prefer, doctor?

RAMBAM: I thank you, but your staff attended to my refreshment while I was awaiting the summons to your presence.

RICHARD: One can't do without some refreshment in this heat. But who wants to drink while he has ripe pears and peaches to feast on? (*He stretches a hand into the basket and withdraws it.*) What's this? All gone? Then we shall have to drink after all!

RAMBAM: The fruit is finished? (RICHARD *nods ruefully.*) But you have not yet exhausted my master's bounty, as you will find if you remove the silken cloth on which the fruit was laid.

[*He does so and lifts out a plain leaden casket.*

RICHARD: What have we here? A weighty object! (*He opens it and gasps.*) Guess what's inside, Madam?

BERENGARIA: Let me see. (*Peering in.*) Whatever is it?

RICHARD: Unmelted snow, my dear! Look, Hubert!

RAMBAM: It is to cool your drinks!

BERENGARIA: Real snow!

RAMBAM: Transported from Mount Hermon by dromedary. (*Slyly.*) And no drugs in it!

RICHARD : (*looking round*): Where is that jug of wine?

BERENGARIA (*taking a jug from the other side-table*): Where you left it, dear. But it's almost empty.

RICHARD (*bawling*): Abdal! (*The dervish springs to life.*) Take the jug away, and fill it—quickly!

[ABDAL *hastens to obey. In passing* RAMBAM, *their eyes meet for a moment in mutual recognition.* ABDAL *takes the jug and hurries out.*

RAMBAM: This is strange! Your dervish's face is familiar to me.

RICHARD: What, Abdal—my runner?

RAMBAM: If I am right, he was one of my first patients in Cairo, many years ago.

RICHARD: Well, he's a good boy. I wouldn't be without him. At my beck and call night and day—I'll be hanged if I know how he manages to eat or sleep. Blondel, my minstrel, discovered him for me.

RAMBAM (*interested*): How did that happen?

RICHARD: They met on the battlefield. Blondel found him wandering—and mistook him for a spy. Then Abdal saved his life—or was it the other way round? Anyway, Blondel brought him along to me—the very man I was looking for! Now the two of them work as a team. (ABDAL *re-enters with the replenished jug.*) Ah, here comes that jug. (ABDAL *brings it to him.*) Good boy. Just leave it on the table. (*He does so.*) You can go back to your place. (ABDAL *obeys.*) And now for the snow! (*He opens the casket and gloats.*)

BERENGARIA: Shall I help you?

RICHARD: No, leave it to me. (*He proceeds to stuff the snow into the jug.*) Now we shall have to wait till it's melted. (*He puts the jug and the casket aside.*) What were you saying about Cairo, doctor? That you once practised medicine there?

RAMBAM: I have talked too much about myself.

RICHARD: Not at all. You are doing me good—helping me to regain my strength: by your own prescription! Besides you seem to have had an uncommonly interesting life. Don't you agree, Hubert?

HUBERT (*dryly*): I agree about the need for getting your strength back, Sir.

BERENGARIA: And I would like to hear more about the doctor's travels. Did you meet with any exciting adventures after you left Spain?

RAMBAM (*firmly*): Nothing of importance, Madam. But I will tell you a little about my work in Cairo if you wish.

RICHARD: Your work as a doctor? The first one I've met who seems to know what he's talking about!

RAMBAM: My medical practice is only a small part of my work, Sir—the least important, perhaps, though I have written a few textbooks.

BERENGARIA (*mildly thrilled*): You write books!

RAMBAM: Too many, I sometimes think.

HUBERT: On what other subjects besides medicine, then?

RAMBAM: Shall I joke with you, and say Astronomy, Physics, Mathematics, Law, Philosophy—?

HUBERT (*not amused*): You have a taste for joking, it seems!

RICHARD: He is making me dizzy!

BERENGARIA: But which is your favourite subject, doctor?

RICHARD: Has that snow melted yet? (*He pours out some wine and sips it.*) Yes, it's quite cold. (*He fills the cup, drinks again, then hands it to his wife.*) Try a sip! (*She tries, and nods her head, whereupon he takes back the cup and drains it.*) The only good drink I've had for months!

BERENGARIA: Will you not invite the doctor to taste it?

RICHARD: Of course. Hubert too. (*Calling.*) Two more cups, Abdal!

BERENGARIA: We have cups here already (*indicating them*).

RICHARD (*calling again*): As you were, boy! (ABDAL *resumes his seat.*)

BERENGARIA: Shall I pour out? (*He assents.*) And one for myself?

RICHARD: Whyever not? (*As she proceeds to do the honours.*) And we'll all drink to the good health of my enemy

E

Saladin, and the confusion of brother John, cousin Philip of France, Leopold of Austria and the rest of my treacherous Christian Allies in the—what do they call it, Hubert? —Diaspora! Is that right?

⌊*He raises his cup, the others raise theirs, and all drink.*

RAMBAM (*quietly*): May I now venture to propose another toast? (*raising his cup*): To all children of Abraham!

[*They respond without enthusiasm.*

HUBERT: Our visitor, it seems, is interested in theology.

RICHARD: That's no subject for a fighting man! (*To* RAMBAM.) Your books are written for scholars, I suppose?

RAMBAM: They are intended for all who can read, Sir.

RICHARD (*with a laugh*): My wife can read!

RAMBAM (*seriously*): Then my books are intended for Her Majesty.

BERENGARIA: Which is the most popular of them?

[RICHARD *pours himself out another cup of wine.*

RAMBAM: It is called "A Guide to the Perplexed".

RICHARD: Who are the perplexed? (*He drinks.*)

RAMBAM: Most serious-minded people.

RICHARD: What are they perplexed about?

RAMBAM: The nature of God, Sir.

RICHARD (*draining his cup*): Theology again. That's Hubert's department.

RAMBAM (*respectfully*): Hubert Walter is a High Priest of your Church?

RICHARD: Bishop of Salisbury, at present. But he'll go higher than that! We'll make him Archbishop of Canterbury yet! (HUBERT *exhibits humble astonishment.*)

RAMBAM: He will then be the head of your English Church?

RICHARD: And no man ever laboured more faithfully for the prize.

HUBERT (*mumbling*): Only my duty, Sir.

RICHARD (*to* RAMBAM): Don't you believe him! He doesn't know his own worth! Where should I have been today without my right-hand man? Leading a great army to the other end of the world is one thing; finding the money for it quite another! Hubert found that money for me. To this day I don't know how he managed it and where it all came from. (*Responding to* HUBERT'*s signals of distress.*) Well, if it offends your modesty, I'll say no more.

BERENGARIA (*in a clear voice*): Please, I would like to hear about the nature of God.

RAMBAM: Perhaps I should be silent in the presence of a Lord Bishop.

HUBERT (*welcoming a change of subject*): You may speak freely, Sir. I would not wish to deter you from gratifying Her Majesty's curiosity.

BERENGARIA: It is not curiosity. (*Almost fiercely.*) It is a strong longing—and despairing—in my heart.

RAMBAM (*surprised*): You are a true seeker, I believe.

BERENGARIA: Oh Sir, I am an ignorant and unhappy woman. I am not of your religion, but if you could give me from your book a word of comfort—in simple language— (*She cannot continue.*)

RAMBAM (*turning to her*): God is near to everyone who turns to Him. He is found by anyone who seeks Him diligently, no matter what his or her religion may be.

[RICHARD, *helping himself to the wine, is savouring another cooling drink.* HUBERT, *with an eye on him, shows increasing impatience.*

HUBERT (*frowning on* RAMBAM): What is this? You are not, I hope, suggesting to Her Majesty that all religions are of equal validity?

RAMBAM (*earnestly*): But can it be doubted, Sir, that saints of all religions are equally acceptable to God? That is what I am suggesting. (*More quietly.*) The intuition first dawned on me while I was conversing with a young Moslem student—(*he breaks off with a start*). But now it all comes back to me! The young Muslim—(*he looks round to glance at the* DERVISH) is in this tent.

HUBERT (*his patience exhausted*): How much longer—? This is not to be endured! (*Losing all control of himself, he throws himself on the ground before* RICHARD, *who has not been listening.*) Your Majesty must bear with me! I implore you to give heed—

[*He lowers his voice, and* RICHARD *is drawn, against his will, to listen. They go into a huddle.* BERENGARIA, *shaken by* RAMBAM'*s words to her, is now deep in her own thoughts.*

RAMBAM (*addressing her after some hesitation*): Would Your Majesty allow me to take the opportunity of renewing an old friendship? (*As she nods assent he goes over to* ABDAL, *and sits beside him.*) It is the same Abdal—once my patient and friend.

ABDAL (*hardly stirring*): I have not forgotten. There was understanding between us.

RAMBAM: Do you remember our last talk before you left Cairo? We spoke about the two Holy Books—our Bible and your Koran.

ABDAL: Also about Abraham and his two sons. You showed me where it was written that Abraham loved both Ishmael and Isaac, how he delighted in them as children, and blessed each before he died. And how they were reunited at his burial.

RAMBAM: And you wept because the children of Israel had been cast out of the Holy Land. And you said you hoped a time would come when the seed of both sons would share peaceably between them the land of their common ancestor.

ABDAL (*with a sigh*): It will come. (*A pause.*) Afterwards I spoke to you of my hope to be accepted as a pupil in a School of Dervishes.

RAMBAM (*looking hard at him*): You found a teacher, I think.

ABDAL: He had been waiting for me to find him.

RAMBAM: Yes. I noticed the patch on the robe you are wearing. So you became a Sufi.

ABDAL: You know about the Way?

RAMBAM: Not much goes on that does not reach my ear. You are on active service, I surmise—in quest, perhaps, of the Fruits of Heaven.

BERENGARIA (*suddenly, raising her head*): Richard! (*He does not hear her.*)

ABDAL: And you—are now in the service of Sultan Saladin. (*He pauses.*) Saladin has talks with Sufi masters. Did you know that?

RAMBAM: Yes. He was visited by one lately. (*Softly.*) Some of your teachers procure miracles?

ABDAL: We do not speak of that.

RAMBAM: Rightly. But miracles happen. The spirit of God moves upon the water.

BERENGARIA (*more loudly*): Richard! I have a wonderful idea!

RAMBAM (*to* ABDAL): I must leave you, brother.

[*He returns to his former position as* RICHARD *suddenly breaks away from* HUBERT.

RICHARD (*distraught*): Yes, I hear you, Hubert, I hear you! But if I listen any longer I shall go mad! Yes, I prefer, if you like, to fritter away precious time listening to a farrago of nonsense! Do you want to bring on my fever again? Where is doctor Rambam?

RAMBAM: Here, Sir.

RICHARD: That book you spoke of—your "Guide to the Perplexed"—if ever a man had need of it, I am that man! (*He laughs.*) I can see only one way out of my perplexities. If you will ask Saladin to release you from his service, I invite you to enter mine, and to return to England with me as my court physician.

RAMBAM (*recoiling*): You cannot be serious, Sir.

BERENGARIA (*excitedly*): But, Richard—that was my great idea! I have been trying to attract your attention. Oh, doctor, if you will only consent to come and live with us, and be our guide!

RAMBAM (*in his own perplexity*): But I have a wife and small son in Cairo—

RICHARD: I will take care of you all! I give you my personal guarantee for your safety and welfare throughout my realm!

RAMBAM (*dryly*): The climate of England would not suit us, I fear.

RICHARD (*uneasily*): You have heard reports of the ugly scenes that marred my coronation in London? Nothing in my whole life ever caused me more distress and anger.

RAMBAM: I can believe you, Sir. I know the Jews of England served you well.

RICHARD: And are hated by the common folk for no better reason. But I would make amends for the past. . . . Why not give England a chance? You might promote a better understanding between my people and yours.

RAMBAM: That is a temptation. But how would our poor Cairo Jewry fare without the leader of their community?

HUBERT (*more calmly*): Moreover, Sir— (*with withering emphasis*) we are still at war!

RICHARD (*recovering himself*): And I have been dreaming— or raving! (*He rubs his eyes.*) We are still at war. And our parley must have an end. (*His eye falls on the basket. He turns to* RAMBAM.) I am grateful to Saladin for his friendly gesture. Thanks to his physician, I am again fighting fit, and the war goes on. (*He calls.*) Abdal, remove this basket.

[ABDAL *jumps to it, comes forward, and carries the basket away.*

BERENGARIA (*from the heart*): Oh God! Help us all!

ABDAL (*stopping on his way out*): Sir, there is something left in the basket.

RICHARD: What? A piece of fruit in one of the corners?

ABDAL: No, Sir. A missive at the bottom! (*He holds it up.*)

RICHARD (*with a shrug*): Saladin's compliments, I suppose. Give it to me. (*As* ABDAL *hands him the document.*) H'm, it is sealed! (*He breaks the seal, commences to read, and is astounded.*) Hubert!

HUBERT (*hurrying to his side*): What is it, Sir?

RICHARD (*reading*): "My Final Terms." (*He looks up.*) Read it for me. My eyes are swimming. (*He hands him the letter.*) Give me the gist—and your counsel.

HUBERT (*after a careful reading*): The terms are not unreasonable in my judgement.

RICHARD: Not unreasonable? What of Ascalon?

HUBERT: He will agree to demolish the fortifications if we cede it.

RICHARD: I will not cede it.

HUBERT: He also agrees to indemnify you against the cost of the fortifications. (*A pause.*) Sir, what good would Ascalon be to you, after our armies have left?

RICHARD (*lips compressed*): I will not cede Ascalon. Anything more?

HUBERT: We are to keep all the coastal cities down to Jaffa. And our pilgrims to have free access to all the Holy Places. (*A pause.*) His Final Terms.

RICHARD (*wavering*): You think we should accept?

HUBERT: Yes, Sir.

RICHARD (*briefly*): Have it your own way.

   [*In the general release of tension,* BERENGARIA *comes slowly forward to confront* RAMBAM.

BERENGARIA (*almost in a whisper*): This has been your doing, I think.

RAMBAM (*shaking his head*): These are my hands, Madam. For the doing of things, look elsewhere.

[*She returns to her place, pondering.*

RICHARD: When you see Saladin, doctor, tell him I hope to return next year and win the remainder of Palestine back from him.

RAMBAM: I know what his reply will be, Sir. (RICHARD *grunts.*) That if he has to lose the land in the end, he would rather it were won by King Richard than by any other Prince in the world. (*He bows.*) Good health, and good hearts (*he looks hard at the Queen*) to both your Majesties! (*He turns to go.*)

RICHARD: You will see to his comforts, Hubert.

RAMBAM: Pray, Sir, do not trouble his Grace. Could you spare your dervish to bring me to my horse?

RICHARD: Go with him, Abdal. And send Blondel to me.

RAMBAM (*going off with* ABDAL): Another of those miracles, brother?

[*Exeunt* RAMBAM *and* ABDAL.

RICHARD: Hubert, you will have to see that my wife and sister sail from Acre to reach France before the winter storms. (*To his wife.*) Will you go and prepare Joanna? No dilly-dallying, mind!

BERENGARIA: Yes, Richard. Oh, thank God, thank God!

[*She goes out in tears.*

RICHARD: I must set my affairs in order quickly, and start as soon after the ladies as possible. (BLONDEL *enters with his harp.*) Ah, there you are, Blondel. You can play to me while I wash and dress—give me strength for what more has to be done today. (BLONDEL *sits and strikes three notes on his harp.*) Hubert, your helping hand under my back. (*Abruptly.*) Where's Abdal? (*With* HUBERT's *support, his naked body is beginning to rise above the sheet, as* ABDAL *re-enters the tent.*) Abdal, come and wash my stinking body.

CURTAIN

SHYLOCK'S END

A Dream Play in One Act

To Hilary

CHARACTERS

THE JUGGLER

ANTONIO

LORENZO

JESSICA

TUBAL

NERISSA

GRATIANO

SHYLOCK

PORTIA

Produced by Charles Lefeaux, and transmitted by B.B.C., Radio 4, on 8 September 1970 with the following cast:

THE JUGGLER	Andrew Sachs
ANTONIO	Hector Ross
LORENZO	Malcolm Hayes
JESSICA	Valerie Kirkbright
TUBAL	Leonard Fenton
NERISSA	Kathleen Helme
GRATIANO	Clifford Norgate
SHYLOCK	John Gabriel
PORTIA	Margaret Wolfit
LUTENIST	David Channon

SHYLOCK'S END

On a long bench, in a deserted street, Antonio, *sombrely dressed, lean and care-worn, sits meditating. Standing over him, the* Juggler, *clad in multi-coloured jester's gown, his face masked under a large hat with turned-up brim, holds a wand raised like a conductor's baton.*

At a signal from him, soft music off, gradually subsiding.

Juggler (*murmurs*): "In sooth I know not why I am so sad."

Antonio (*starting*): What's that?

Juggler (*evenly*): Those are the opening words of a comedy.

Antonio: I seem to have heard them before.

Juggler: The comedy is "The Merchant of Venice"; the speaker, the Merchant, Antonio.

Antonio: My name is Antonio. I am a merchant of Venice of long standing.

Juggler: Then perhaps you are the subject of the comedy. Do you trade in cargoes carried by your argosies to all parts of the world?

Antonio: I do.

Juggler: And are you a bachelor?

Antonio: I am.

Juggler: Had you a friend of noble birth, Bassanio by name, a young spendthrift who, with your financial assistance, wooed and won the hand of a young and beautiful heiress? And were you prepared to sacrifice your life in addition to your fortune, on Bassanio's behalf?

ANTONIO: All this is true.

JUGGLER: Were you, in consequence, subjected to a harrowing ordeal, from which—surviving a diabolical plot against your life—you preserved both body and wealth intact, while witnessing the fall and humiliation of your enemy, a Jewish usurer? (ANTONIO *nods assent.*) All these were the ingredients of the comedy.

ANTONIO (*sighing wearily*): And the comedy is ended.

JUGGLER: Are you so sure of that? You are as sad now as ever.

ANTONIO: Sadder.

JUGGLER: Can you explain that?

ANTONIO (*rousing himself, with a start*): Who are you?

JUGGLER: That is a good question.

ANTONIO: (*in sudden awe*): Are you my maker?

JUGGLER: No, I do not make. But I am in His service. I help to sort things out. I am the Juggler.

ANTONIO: I see.

JUGGLER: I am part of a philosophical machine. I put questions, and find answers. I am known to students of Cabala, Alchemy, Magic, Astrology—

ANTONIO (*trembling, and crossing himself*): That will be quite enough.

JUGGLER: Do not alarm yourself. This is only a dream.

ANTONIO (*mopping his brow*): Oh, a dream—that of course, makes all the difference. Strange things happen quite naturally in dreams. Is it a friendly dream?

JUGGLER: All dreams are friends.

ANTONIO: Then I will listen carefully.

JUGGLER: And answer my questions?

ANTONIO: Certainly.

JUGGLER: Tell me then what has happened since your victory over Shylock.

ANTONIO: Bassanio has married Portia. That is what has happened.

JUGGLER: That is why you are still so sad?

ANTONIO: Certainly.

JUGGLER: You have not seen Bassanio since his marriage?

ANTONIO (*glumly*): I do not expect to see him again. (*He pauses.*) His time is fully occupied in Belmont, I know. (*Another pause.*) What with the care and management of his wife's estate—and the exhausting pursuits of a country gentleman—

JUGGLER: You do not reproach him for neglecting you?

ANTONIO (*doggedly*): I love him still, as I loved him from the first.

JUGGLER: Unselfishly?

ANTONIO: That is the point.

JUGGLER: "Greater love hath no man than this, that a man lay down his life for his friend."

ANTONIO: So it stands in Holy writ.

JUGGLER: And have you no other interest in life?

ANTONIO: "Where the heart is, there shall your treasure be."

JUGGLER: Is your heart not in your mercantile business?

ANTONIO (*emphatically*): It never has been. I am no representative merchant of Venice.

JUGGLER: You have the heart, rather, of a poet?

ANTONIO: You perceive that? You have discovered my secret.

JUGGLER: In your element, you would be writing sonnets?

ANTONIO: That is the form I would choose.

JUGGLER: "Let me not to the marriage of true minds
            Admit impediment. Love is not love
            That alters when it alteration finds
            Or bends with the remover to remove—"

ANTONIO: You take the words out of my mouth!

JUGGLER: The fact that your friend has dropped you makes no difference to your love?

ANTONIO: None whatever. (*Bravely.*) By that faith I live.

JUGGLER: And should you ever lose that faith—?

ANTONIO (*vehemently*): I will not hear of the possibility.

JUGGLER: Yet the fear of it enters your mind occasionally?

ANTONIO (*with a groan*): It has haunted me every day since—since—

JUGGLER: Since a young nobleman smiled on a merchant poet and the affair began.

ANTONIO (*emotionally*): "Love is not love that alteration finds!"

JUGGLER (*shortly*): Life goes on, however.

ANTONIO: Not for me. I have no further use for life. For me, the comedy is ended—as I have told you.

JUGGLER: And for your fellows?

ANTONIO (*contemptuously*): My fellows!

JUGGLER: You are not the only character in the comedy. (*Severely.*) Have you forgotten Shylock? What has happened to him since the Judgment?

ANTONIO: I neither know nor care. Am I Shylock's keeper? I have no hard feelings. I am simply indifferent to his existence.

JUGGLER: And what of the other members of your old circle—Lorenzo and Jessica, Gratiano and Nerissa? And what of Portia?

ANTONIO: All married—all dead to me! I have washed my hands of them!

JUGGLER: You will have to think again, friend.

[*He waves his wand, and the scene fades into a blackout. When the light returns, the* JUGGLER *has disappeared.* ANTONIO *is still seated on the bench brooding.*

ANTONIO: I must think again, he said.

[*Enter* LORENZO, *handsomely attired, looking about him.*

LORENZO (*swooping to his quarry*): Antonio! At last I've run you to earth! Why are you not on the Rialto? I've been hunting for you everywhere! (ANTONIO *stares at him.*) You have not forgotten me, I hope?

ANTONIO (*unhappily*): No, I haven't forgotten. (*With forced heartiness.*) You and your charming Jessica are as high-spirited as ever?

LORENZO: Not having seen her lately I cannot answer for Jessica. As for myself—(*he clears his throat ominously*) I hope to be in better spirits after taking up a few moments of your valuable time.

ANTONIO (*gloomily*): What can I do for you?

LORENZO: Lend me three thousand ducats, old man—and so help me out of an unfortunate predicament. Let me tell you about it. (*He seats himself beside the squirming* ANTONIO.) It's for a musical project. You remember my passion for new music. You shared it yourself, I believe? (*This is news to* ANTONIO.) I've just come back from Florence where the young progressive musicians have achieved a positive miracle—discovered a new dimension in music! It's the most important artistic event since the days of that other Lorenzo, the Magnificent! This is a multiple art—music fused with poetry and dramatic action—recovering the whole secret of ancient Greek tragedy. Think of it, Antonio! And I've arranged to organize a Venetian Music Festival—under the patronage of the Duke, if I can fix it—and transport everybody and everything from Florence, to give Venice a full-scale experimental production of the musical art of the future! The only catch of course, is the colossal expense which I have personally guaranteed. Sheer lunacy! However, I can't back out of it now, and I reckon that, with the 3,000 ducats from you, I should be able to scrape through somehow or other.

ANTONIO (*stiffly*): I am sorry to have to disappoint an old friend—(LORENZO *recoils*) but I am not in a position to lend you the money.

LORENZO: What do you mean—not in a position? You can raise it, can't you?

ANTONIO: I have given my answer.

LORENZO: Then may I remind you that you are holding money of mine—very much more than 3,000 ducats—

ANTONIO (*bewildered*): What money are you talking about?

LORENZO: Shylock's money which was paid to you as my trustee. You surely haven't forgotten the Deed of Gift?

ANTONIO (*helplessly*): It comes back to me. (*He buries his head in his hands.*)

[JESSICA, *well painted, gowned and bejewelled, sneaks in from the back and, unperceived, stands listening.*

LORENZO: Old Shylock won't live for ever, so you might just as well pay out the money now, while I can make good use of it. Charge me interest, if you like.

ANTONIO (*flaring up*): How dare you insult me!

[JESSICA *has difficulty in suppressing her mirth.*

LORENZO: You surely didn't think I meant that seriously, old man. Everyone in Venice knows and respects your scruples. And as if I should offer to pay interest on my own money!

JESSICA (*coming forward*): On whose money, did you say?

[*The two men rise to their feet, equally disconcerted.*

ANTONIO: Jessica!

LORENZO (*nastily*): You remember the Jew's daughter? (*Addressing her.*) I understood we were not supposed to be on speaking terms. (*To* ANTONIO.) There has been, you might say, a rift in the domestic lute.

JESSICA: I have come to speak to my Trustee.

LORENZO: You mean, *my* Trustee.

ANTONIO (*with distaste*): Must you embroil me in your quarrel?

JESSICA: Yes. Perhaps you haven't heard the news—either of you.

ANTONIO (*loftily*): I hear no news.

LORENZO: I have been away in Florence. What news?

JESSICA: News of my unrespected father.

LORENZO (*hopefully*): Is he dead?

JESSICA: The next best thing. He is dying.

ANTONIO (*taken aback*): Shylock—dying?

LORENZO (*cheerfully*): That should simplify everything!

ANTONIO: You have come from his bedside?

JESSICA: Is it likely! (*tensely*) Antonio, I want to see that Deed of Gift.

ANTONIO: Was it not given to Lorenzo?

JESSICA: Yes, by Portia. And Lorenzo says he gave it to you.

LORENZO (*lamely*): Either that or I have lost it.

JESSICA: I might have known you were lying! But at least Antonio still holds the money, I hope?

LORENZO: He holds it in trust for me.

JESSICA: I challenge that. I am Shylock's daughter.

LORENZO: And I am Shylock's daughter's husband. So long as we are man and wife, your property is under my control.

JESSICA: And you can play the fool with my father's money? Don't you let him have a single ducat, Antonio! I'm warning you: I stand for the law.

ANTONIO (*on pins and needles*): The law must be respected. Let me think: the terms of the trust must have followed the Judge's directions.

JESSICA: I was not present in court—unfortunately. (*Looking at* LORENZO.) I was at Belmont all that day—with him. (*Suddenly she shudders.*)

LORENZO: You need not remind me . . . (*roughly*) everyone knows what the Judge directed. The money was to pass, on Shylock's death, "Unto his son Lorenzo and his daughter". In that order.

JESSICA: Implying "so long as they are living together".

LORENZO: Who says so?

JESSICA: My lawyer. (*Both men recoil.*) And it is he who will demand to see the Deed.

LORENZO (*angrily*): You've gone to a lawyer? Are you crazy?

ANTONIO: This is intolerable!

JESSICA (*calmly*): According to my lawyer, Antonio may be required to exercise a Trustee's discretion—whatever that may mean. (ANTONIO *reels slightly*.) But he thinks the whole trust may be bad in law, in which case the money is still Shylock's, and will come to me as his next of kin. If only my father had engaged a good lawyer to represent him at the trial, none of this trouble would have arisen.

LORENZO (*gasping*): Well, for cool, shameless effrontery—what do you say to that, Antonio?

ANTONIO (*wearily*): I have nothing further to say to either of you. (*He returns to the seat, where he endeavours to isolate himself from their company.*)

LORENZO (*rounding on JESSICA*): And I have only this to say to my bloody-minded spouse: if you want a fight you shall have it, but be careful to come into court with clean hands! I've been hearing all about your little adventures while I was away in Florence.

JESSICA (*flinching*): What have you heard?

LORENZO: I may play the fool with your father's money, but who's been playing the whore?

JESSICA (*defiantly*): Easier said than proved in Court!

LORENZO (*violently*): Stinking little painter boys and gondoliers—I have the names and criminal records of all of them, including your latest catch, Piero the pimp!

[JESSICA *flies at him with clenched fists and they struggle furiously.*

ANTONIO (*beside himself*): They are driving me mad! (*He shuts his eyes and covers his ears as the scene begins to darken. Then, despairingly.*) Lorenzo, Jessica—hear me! You have been lovers at Belmont—so short a time ago! Can you have forgotten? That evening, in the moonlight, with the music whispering through the trees, and the exchange of vows in mutual trust— Are you the same two people?

[*Only a faint suggestion of moonlight now relieves the darkness, while* LORENZO *and* JESSICA *still go through the motions of their struggle. The outline of the* JUGGLER *appears behind them waving his wand, to the accompaniment of soft music. At his first words, the combatants separate, and cower on either side.*

JUGGLER (*impressively*):
  Sit, Jessica. Look how the floor of heaven
  Is thick inlaid with patens of bright gold.
  There's not the smallest orb which thou behold'st
  But in his motion like an angel sings
  Still choiring to the young-eyed cherubims;
  Such harmony is in immortal souls!
  But whilst this muddy vesture of decay
  Doth grossly close it in, we cannot hear it.

  [*The moonlight fades out. On the darkened stage* LORENZO
  and JESSICA *are just discernible.*

JESSICA and LORENZO (*echoing, simultaneously, in despair*):
      Such harmony is in immortal souls!
      But whilst this muddy vesture of decay
      Doth grossly close it in, we cannot hear it.

  [*Their shadowy figures are seen to rise and mechanically
  resume the battle.*

JUGGLER (*gently*): Antonio, yes, they are the same two
people. Swinging between the opposites of Heaven and
Hell. So are you all. Lorenzo, Jessica, Antonio, Shylock.
That is perhaps the first lesson.

  [*Blackout. Soft music swells again briefly before the light
  returns.* ANTONIO *is sitting alone on the bench, brooding, as
  on his first appearance. Presently,* TUBAL, *a Jew, in his late
  fifties, wearing the yellow cap of the ghetto, enters to cross the
  stage.* ANTONIO *looks up as he passes, and calls.*

ANTONIO: Master Tubal! (TUBAL *halts, stands rigid.*) Were
you not one of Shylock's friends?

TUBAL: Tubal is my name. (*He does not turn.*)

ANTONIO: Shylock is dying, I hear.

TUBAL (*controlled*): I have not heard it.

ANTONIO: Have you seen him lately?

TUBAL: Not since he left us. (*He moves slowly on.*)

ANTONIO: Master Tubal. (*He stops.*) Do you know me?

TUBAL: Yes (*bitterly*), Signor Antonio.

ANTONIO (*rising impulsively*): Stay a moment, I pray you. (TUBAL *hesitates.*) I have been reflecting on my former behaviour to Shylock—and to all of you. I recall it with horror and shame. Will you sit down for a moment and hear me?

TUBAL: How can I refuse? (ANTONIO *bows him to the bench.*)

ANTONIO (*sitting beside him*): Let me make full confession. (TUBAL *looks round fearfully.*) You would rather not be seen in my company? I understand. I will be brief. (*He pauses.*) I have been asking myself this question: which is the merchant and which the Jew? What is the difference between us? Both are in business to make money: if love of money be the root of all evil, we are equally tainted. I railed at Shylock only to conceal from myself that we were brothers in sin. Do you follow?

TUBAL (*bitterly*): A Jew may only live in Venice by practising usury.

ANTONIO: I knew that too. In hating Shylock, I was both hating and deceiving myself. I even imagined I was a good Christian.

TUBAL (*grudgingly*): You showed true love for your friend. That was good.

ANTONIO: Was it? It was love nourished on hatred for others, and so poisoned. And it was that hatred that roused Shylock's hatred in return. Only he paid the penalty for both of us.

TUBAL: We have a word for it in the Bible: scapegoat . . . And yet, if only you could have seen—how poor Shylock sought your friendship.

ANTONIO: Is that possible?

TUBAL: Recall, Sir. You came to him asking for a loan of 3,000 ducats, not as a friend—friends do not charge interest—but as a declared enemy: you made no secret of it. And how did he receive the request? Did he not at at once offer to lend the money free of interest—proposing as a poor jest, to cover his shyness in returning a soft answer to brutal insolence, a preposterous bargain which no one could have expected to become enforceable; for all your rich argosies were at sea, and no danger in sight. The offer of his friendship was sincere. There was no plot to trap you. All the mischief was made by unforeseeable events: on your side a coincidence of business disasters, on his, the defection of his daughter turned traitor and thief. Shylock went mad, and only then remembered the "merry bond"—

ANTONIO: I am even more to blame than I had thought.

TUBAL (*turning away*): I was much to blame for what followed.

ANTONIO: How so?

TUBAL: I was criminally guilty. Infected with Shylock's madness, I and other friends egged him on to avenge all our grievances on a single enemy seemingly in his power. We fed his madness.

ANTONIO: All hatred is mad. And hatred, it seems, is in all of us—and the scapegoat pays!

TUBAL: And now Shylock is dying, you say. Who is caring for him? By some miracle his daughter? (ANTONIO *shakes his head*.) Then strangers. Since he left us, he may be anywhere.

ANTONIO: You have not seen or heard from him since?

TUBAL: He disappeared after his baptism. A rumour reached us that he had entered a home for converted Jews: (*sadly*) it may even be true.

ANTONIO: I was responsible for his baptism. Can you believe that it was well-meant?

TUBAL: I would find it difficult to believe.

ANTONIO: Our church teaches that it is a necessary starting point for salvation.

TUBAL (*dryly*): Also that Christianity is a religion of love.

ANTONIO: It is that or nothing.

TUBAL: Do you believe it is good to convert a man to your religion by force?

ANTONIO: I— I— (*he gives it up*) I neither believe nor disbelieve. I now question so many of the things I have always taken for granted. (*Pondering*.) Portia might provide the right answer.

TUBAL: Portia? Who may Portia be?

[*A young matron has arrived on the scene.*

NERISSA (*her name*): I can tell you that, Sir. She is a doer of good deeds in a naughty world. (*Coming forward*.) And who am I? One who has been privileged to serve that Lady since childhood.

ANTONIO (*rising astonished*): Nerissa! Or can I be mistaken?

NERISSA: Nerissa is still my name.

ANTONIO: And you are still in Portia's service?

TUBAL (*rising nervously*): I must take my leave.

NERISSA (*politely*): And who might you be, Sir?

ANTONIO: He is a former friend of Shylock's.

NERISSA: And what was the question asked, which was to be referred to my mistress?

TUBAL (*boldly*): I asked how it can possibly benefit a man to be baptized against his will.

NERISSA: Are you perhaps Master Tubal?

TUBAL (*taken aback*): You know my name?

NERISSA: Your old friend has often spoken of you.

TUBAL: Shylock? Then you can tell us of him? Is it true that he is dying? And where is he now staying?

ANTONIO: And you can tell us perhaps what happened to him after— after—?

NERISSA: You had better be seated again, gentlemen—and let me sit between you— (*she seats herself accordingly*) and I will tell you what I can. (*When all are seated.*) First (*turning to* TUBAL) it is true that our friend has not long to live. Next, he is no longer Shylock. That name was jettisoned at his baptism, which even you, Sir, must allow is a minor benefit. His new name is Samson. (*As* TUBAL's *lips move.*) Your comment?

TUBAL: Samson is not a Christian name.

NERISSA: It was the name chosen for him, by Portia.

ANTONIO: Did Portia then take charge of him?

NERISSA: Not until later. After the christening, he returned to his old house, unaccompanied, I believe.

ANTONIO: You must have seen him, then, Tubal?

TUBAL: He took to his bed, and would see no one. For two days and nights he remained as one dead. Then during the third night he disappeared—from his house, from the ghetto, and, as far as we could ascertain, from Venice. We made enquiries of the civil authorities; fearing that he might have thrown himself into a canal. There was no trace of him.

NERISSA: Now I can take up the story. How or when he left the city we could never discover, but he had wandered many miles beyond the walls—guided by Providence, it would seem, in the direction of Belmont—before his strength gave out. He was found in a field, grovelling on all fours, soaked in dew and eating the grass, declaring that he was the deposed King Nebuchadnezzar.

TUBAL (*distressed*): Out of his wits? It is not to be wondered at!

ANTONIO: Near Belmont, you say?

NERISSA: Some distance from it. But by a strange chance he was found and recognized by a former servant, a simpleton, Lancelot Gobbo by name, now in Portia's service.

ANTONIO: I remember young Gobbo.

NERISSA: Procuring transport as best he could, he managed to bring his old master to Belmont where Portia at once sent for her own doctors, appointed skilled attendants to look after him day and night, and set about restoring both his wits and his health. It has not been easy. None of us can ever know what torments he endured after leaving the court that day. It may have eased his frenzied mind to see himself in fantasy as a king banished and disgraced. (*Smiling*.) When his Nebuchadnezzar fit was on him, nothing would satisfy him but that a young man he called Daniel must be sent for to counsel him. This Daniel was some kind of judge, it seems.

TUBAL: Daniel was a prophet who interpreted King Nebuchadnezzar's dreams.

NERISSA: That was it, then. Well, we always did what we could to humour him. Sometimes we lost hope of ever seeing him in his right senses again. But little by little we pulled him round, as Portia had determined we should. She usually gets her own way.

ANTONIO: And so he was restored to both wits and health?

NERISSA: More or less. But he was not the same man. Broken and mended, you might say, but changed, too—with a new kind of power.

TUBAL: And now he is dying?

ANTONIO: Is he still at Belmont?

NERISSA: No. As soon as he was fit enough, Portia arranged for him to be moved to a small house in Venice—one of her father's properties which happened to be untenanted, and was easily converted into a convalescent home. And there he has remained ever since.

TUBAL (*suspicious*): With other converted Jews?

NERISSA: No, Sir. The only other inhabitants are the Warden and his wife neither of whom are Jews. As the warden's wife, I can vouch for it.

ANTONIO (*in surprise*): Gratiano is the Warden?

NERISSA: Yes, and still my husband. The post suits us both, which is not surprising as Gratiano had been unemployed since our marriage, and before it! Portia's helping hand has been everywhere. But the strangest part is—this new power I was speaking of in the man once known as Shylock. You might say it was a miracle. I think, when you first saw me just now you did not recognize the old Nerissa. You will find it the same with my husband. Did you ever encounter Gratiano in the old days, Master Tubal?

TUBAL (*grimly*): Yes . . . he was the most ferocious of all the Jew-baiters. And Shylock, you say, is in this man's charge?

NERISSA: Come and see for yourself. The house is not far away.

TUBAL (*with deliberation*): Yes, I would like to visit my old friend before he dies.

NERISSA: And he would be glad to receive a visit from you, I know.

ANTONIO: Could he bear, do you think, to see Antonio, face to face again?

NERISSA: It is what he has been hoping for, I know. Come, both of you.

[*As they follow her, the light fades. Blackout and music. When the light returns, the scene has changed to an interior simply furnished as a parlour. No one is in occupation. Then* NERISSA *enters, followed by* ANTONIO *and* TUBAL.

NERISSA: This is our home. And here my husband comes (GRATIANO, *clad with respectable dignity, has entered from a side door*) to greet us. (*She embraces him.*) The patient sleeps, Gratiano?

GRATIANO: Soundly. You have brought visitors, Nerissa.
(*Going to them.*) I bid you welcome, gentlemen ... (*starting*)
Antonio! (*They clasp hands, and he turns to* TUBAL.) You,
Sir? I seem to know your face.

TUBAL (*stiffly*): A friend of Shylock. Tubal is my name.

GRATIANO (*averting his eyes*): I am ashamed when I
remember ...

TUBAL (*coldly*): I have come to see Shylock before he dies.

GRATIANO: He should be waking soon. Will you be seated.
(*He obeys.*)

NERISSA (*breaking an awkward silence*): I'll leave you—to be
by him when he wakes. (*She withdraws into the side room. The
embarrassment increases.*)

GRATIANO (*approaching Antonio*): We meet, old friend, in
altered circumstances. (*They inspect each other.*) More
wrinkles! We grow no younger. As for me— (*suddenly
seizing him by the arm, he marches him off*) I hope to God I am
not the swine I used to be. (*They turn about.*) What say you
to that, Second Gentleman?

ANTONIO (*entering into the spirit*): I say, First Gentleman,
that if a man does not make efforts to amend his animal
nature and develop his inner potentialities while he lives,
he had better be still-born. (*They turn again.*) I say, moreover, First Gentleman, that Antonio hath for once given
birth to a kind of witticism: Ha, ha! (*They share the joke,
then abruptly break apart and relapse into the former lull.*)

GRATIANO (*suddenly alert*): He is waking, I think. (*Falling on
his knees.*) Lord, have mercy on us all!

   [*He rises as* NERISSA *enters, pushing a wheelchair on which
   a shrunken, frail old man is lying back, motionless. It is*
   SHYLOCK.

NERISSA (*cheerfully*): Here we come at last to join the company!

SHYLOCK (*opening his eyes, faintly*): Where is my warden?

GRATIANO (*hurrying to his side*): Here! What is it? (SHYLOCK *extends a hand. Taking it.*) Had a good sleep? Feeling more comfortable?

SHYLOCK (*in a shaky voice*): Comfortable. But weak.

GRATIANO: Not too weak to see your visitors?

SHYLOCK (*smiling happily*): Yes. Daniel was coming.

GRATIANO: He is not here yet. But other friends—

NERISSA: I told him, but I don't think he took it in. (*Raising her voice.*) Daniel will be coming later, we hope. Two other gentlemen are here to see you.

SHYLOCK (*disappointment*): Not Daniel?

GRATIANO: One of them is Antonio.

SHYLOCK (*tonelessly*): Antonio? (*starting*) Antonio, did you say? (ANTONIO *comes forward.*) Antonio—from the Rialto? (ANTONIO *stands before him with bowed head.*) Antonio, the man old Shylock would have murdered? (*He gazes at him.*) My sight is not good. . . . Yes, it is he. You have come to visit—then you have forgiven me?

ANTONIO (*hoarsely*): I have come to ask *your* forgiveness. I provoked the hatred between us.

SHYLOCK (*weeping*): Give me—your hand. (*He holds it tightly for a moment, then falls back.* ANTONIO, *at a signal from* NERISSA, *draws aside.*)

NERISSA (*as emotion subsides*): There is another visitor. (*As his face lights up.*) No, not Daniel yet. (*Beckoning.*) Master Tubal.

TUBAL (*stumbling forward*): This cannot be Shylock!

SHYLOCK: Who speaks of Shylock? (TUBAL *reaches his side.*) Why, it is Tubal! (*Gazing at him.*) Are you not ashamed of me? (TUBAL *breaks down.*) Yet you have come at last.

TUBAL (*restraining himself*): None of us knew where to find you.

SHYLOCK (*shaking his head*): Antonio has forgiven Shylock. The Synagogue would forget him.

TUBAL: How could anyone forget? But how—to remember? (*Wringing his hands.*) What am I to report to the Synagogue?

SHYLOCK: Tell them that a Seal of Solomon will be engraved on my tomb.

TUBAL (*with a groan*): After a Christian burial?

SHYLOCK: It was Daniel who thought of it.

TUBAL: It is all beyond my understanding.

SHYLOCK: Is not God himself beyond our understanding? All evil things—wild beasts, unkind daughters, earthquakes—we call them Acts of God. All—beyond our understanding. It may be wisdom to accept.

TUBAL: Even baptism—is that to be accepted?

SHYLOCK: That word of fear! Was not baptism, for our people, a rite of cleansing? And for me it is an image of new life given to one bad Jew. An image—Daniel allows it to be so.

TUBAL: Daniel? Who is this Daniel?

SHYLOCK (*smiling*): A young doctor of law who put Shylock in his place.

TUBAL: What? Not that youth of subtle tongue who destroyed you?

SHYLOCK: Aye, who toppled Shylock into the dust.

TUBAL: And so— (*ironically*) converted him?

SHYLOCK: And so knocked the old man out of him. My benefactor!

TUBAL: And so forced you to desert your own people, ally yourself with our Christian oppressors and their Church?

SHYLOCK: Christian, Church— more words of fear! Words can have many meanings. These words, as words, mean nothing to me. Behind all words is a Reality. (*He closes his eyes, exhausted.*)

TUBAL (*urgently*): But this reality— Hear me further, Shylock!

GRATIANO: Pray you leave him a little while, Sir. He tires so quickly.

NERISSA (*listening*): I hear a carriage at the door.

GRATIANO: Daniel? I will go and see.

[TUBAL *draws back slightly as* GRATIANO *hurries out. Soft music. Then* GRATIANO *returns ushering in* PORTIA *in her wig and legal robes.* ANTONIO *involuntarily moves towards her, as* NERISSA *curtseys deeply. The music ceases.*

PORTIA (*bending over the wheelchair*): He is sleeping, I think. (*She looks round.*) Is it Antonio? Well met! (*They clasp hands.*)

ANTONIO (*huskily*): Bassanio—he is well?

PORTIA: And growing fat! (*More seriously.*) And you—so lean! (*He shrugs.*) But you have found your way here! (*Glancing at* SHYLOCK.) You have spoken to him already? (*He nods.*) And are reconciled? (*He nods again.*) So our prayers are answered! (*Glancing again at* SHYLOCK.) And the end is near.

SHYLOCK (*his eyes still closed*): Daniel, (*before she can answer*) is Tubal still here?

NERISSA (*to* PORTIA, *indicating* TUBAL): Master Tubal is from the synagogue.

[PORTIA, *duly impressed, bows courteously to him.*

TUBAL: I have stayed too long. (*He turns to go.*)

SHYLOCK: Wait yet a moment, Tubal. I ask a favour, Daniel. For Tubal's sake, speak to us of the reality behind our religions. Recall to us those words you spoke in court— (*his voice fails.*)

PORTIA: If memory permits. (*She closes her eyes, then speaks them beautifully.*)

> The quality of mercy is not strained.
> It droppeth as the gentle rain from Heaven
> Upon the place beneath. It is twice blessed.
> It blesseth him that gives, and him that takes.
> 'Tis mightiest in the mightiest. It becomes
> The throned monarch better than his crown—

TUBAL (*sternly*): Pause, and hear me! I accuse the lawyer! (*He proceeds in a shocked silence.*) I was in court, and heard those fine phrases, and was transported by them—as who would not have been? Shylock, as I can testify, was no less moved. Yet you deliberately nullified the effect on him a moment later when you invited him to take his revenge,

*G

and guaranteed him the full authority of the laws of
Venice. That was a lie and you knew it, yet you cunningly
led him into your trap, and slammed the door on him.
There was no mercy in that!

PORTIA (*calmly, in an awful silence*): You have made a fair
point, Master Tubal.

TUBAL: Have you an answer?

GRATIANO (*bending over* SHYLOCK): He is trying to speak.
(*Listening.*) What do you say? (*He nods.*) I will report:
(*To* PORTIA.) "Give them the tale of"—it sounds like the
Arab horsemen.

PORTIA (*smiling*): It is his favourite bed-time fable. (*To*
TUBAL) Will you hear it, Sir? It is quite short.

TUBAL (*with a shrug*): I will hear it.

PORTIA: Once upon a time, there was a man who in his
sleep swallowed a poisonous snake. It stuck in his throat,
and he was very uncomfortable, but did not know what
was wrong with him. A horseman, who was riding by, saw
what had happened, raised his whip, and without hesitation, lashed at the man, paying no heed to his cries for
mercy and his protests that he had done nothing to
deserve such punishment. The horseman continued to
rain blows on him, and at last, when the man had been
beaten almost senseless, the poisonous reptile was thrown
from his stomach. The horseman, having other business to
attend to, then rode on.

[*A short pause. Shylock is feebly gesticulating.*

GRATIANO (*again bending over him*): He says there were
three snakes.

SHYLOCK (*straining to be heard*): Their names were Hatred,
Greed and Pride!

PORTIA (*watching* TUBAL): Master Tubal is not satisfied.

TUBAL: I still say that to practise that mean deception after your plea for mercy was unnecessary hypocrisy. It was the kind of trick they play on spectators in the theatre.

ANTONIO (*innocently*): But wait—surely, or am I dreaming? —this *was* a trick played in the theatre—some comedy about a merchant of Venice.

[*A strangled cry and* SHYLOCK'*s head falls forward.*

PORTIA (*in a clear voice*): Shylock is dead. (*There seems to be some trouble with the lights which flicker uncertainly.* PORTIA *comes forward as the other characters begin to make themselves scarce. But what has happened to her? Somehow, mysteriously, she has been converted into a* PORTIA *with a difference—or could she perhaps be a reincarnated* PORTIA *of the past—none other than bewitching Ellen Terry, once beloved of George Bernard Shaw, whose mischievous influence is surely to be detected in the questionable taste of her peroration?*): Well, as everyone knows perfectly well who I am, I may as well (*throwing off her disguise*) now let my hair down (*she does so*) and acknowledge that Portia was a spoilt child from the first, and has been cheating people all her life, with impunity. My poor father—God bless him—devised a ritual with caskets to save me from becoming the wife of a fortune-hunter, so, in due course, I naturally fell in love with one, and worked the three casket trick so cleverly for his benefit that he married me and has lived happily ever after. Professor Tubal has exposed my fraudulent behaviour in the court, and you will remember that I followed this by swindling my husband out of his wedding ring and his oath. The point is, ladies and gentlemen, that, though incorrigible, I am on the side of the angels, and can do no wrong. And, though I am profoundly ignorant of theology, and know less than nothing about Judaism, you can take it from me that the love I preach is the God of all religions, and keeps you and me on the move. I will now call upon my spiritual husband, Metamorphosis (*enter the* JUGGLER) who is known to students of Cabala, alchemy, astrology, and magic (*the* JUGGLER *bows to her*) to terminate the proceedings. (*She steps back.*)

JUGGLER: Wake up, everybody!

CURTAIN

ACKNOWLEDGMENTS

ROME ON FIRE

My thanks, in particular:

To the Rev. Dr James Parkes, and the Rev. W. W.
Simpson, of the Council of Christians and Jews, for serving
(willy-nilly) as models for heroic characters in a mythical
drama,

To Dr Hugh Schonfield for throwing light on the
situation of Jewish Christians in the early church, and
for correcting some of my mistakes,

To Arnold Toynbee, and his collaborators, in *The
Crucible of Christianity*,

To Dom Gregory Dix for *The Shape of the Liturgy*,

To Patric Dickinson for a line from his translation of
The Aeneid, and, not least,

To the editors and translators of the Penguin Classics
mentioned in the Prologue.

PEACE TALKS IN PALESTINE

For exploiting Steven Runciman's *History of the Crusades* as
my Holinshed, I feel both gratitude and shame. Other
works helpfully consulted were *Richard the Lionheart* by
Kate Norgate, *Maimonides* by Solomon Zeitlin, *The
Source* by James Michener, and *The Way of the Sufi* by
Idries Shah.

SHYLOCK'S END

The story of the Arab Horseman will be found in *Caravan*

of Dreams by Idries Shah, to whom I am deeply indebted for permission to incorporate it in my text.

"The Juggler" is drawn from an interpretation of Tarot cards in P. D. Ouspensky's *A New Model of the Universe*.

Some unfamiliar impressions of *The Merchant of Venice* are reflected from *The Meaning of Shakespeare* by Professor Harold C. Goddard.

H. F. R.